WAITING TO EXIT HELL

THE JOURNEY OUT

DR. KATRINA FERGUSON

WAITING TO EXIT HELL - The Journey Out
By Dr. Katrina Ferguson

Copyright ©2025 - Dr. Katrina Ferguson
All rights reserved.

www.DrKatrinaFerguson.com
www.WaitingToExitHell.com

All Rights Reserved. No part of this publication may be reproduced, stored in a retrieval system, or transmitted in any form by means electronic, mechanical, photocopying, recording or otherwise without prior written permission of the publisher, except as provided by United States of America copyright law.

Unless otherwise noted, all Scripture quotations are from the King James Version®. Used by permission. All rights reserved.

Scripture quotations marked NIV are from the NIV/KJV Parallel Bible, ©1985, by the Zondervan Corporation. Used by permission. All rights reserved.

Scripture quotations marked NKJV are from The Maxwell Leadership Bible, ©2002, by Maxwell Motivation Inc. Used by permission. All rights reserved.

ISBN: 978-0-9981690-5-7
Printed in the United States of America

FIG Publishing * 1500 Beville Rd., #606 394 * Daytona Beach, FL 3211

ACKNOWLEDGEMENT

This book is the result of a deeply personal journey of healing, restoration, and recovery from grief and loss. Its origin lies in the compassionate and persistent support of a dear friend who watched me enter what felt like "hell" following an emotionally painful situation. Not only did he refuse to give up on me, but he also wouldn't allow me to walk through the valley alone. For 21 days straight, he sent me texts filled with encouragement, wisdom, and hope, refusing to rest until he saw me begin to exit that particular "hell."

Through his unwavering support, I began to realize that this wasn't my first encounter with "hell on earth," nor would it be my last. There were multiple situations in my life—from the loss of a parent, loss of a marriage, loss of relationships, and just loss in general—circumstances that left me feeling trapped, confused, broken, and without a clear path forward.

This time was different. I didn't have to walk through this situation on my own. My friend helped me engage in a process that not only guided me out of that particularly dark season, but it became part of my battle equipment to navigate future challenges. It is this plan, developed through prayer, the study of Scripture, and practical actions, which is the foundation of this book.

Studies show that it takes 21 days to form a habit. This is not to say that in 21 days you will be "over it." Let's be clear. The habit will form in 21 days, but it will take another 21 days or so for those habits to become automatic, to become part of who you are. These habits turn into a way of living, creating a roadmap that you can rely on every time you feel yourself encountering emotional or spiritual despair. This journey extended beyond those initial 21 days and has become the 31-day life-changing process that I now want to share with you.

My friend, your unwavering support and friendship will never be forgotten. This book is an extension of that experience, designed to help others form and reinforce habits that lead to healing, restoration, and ultimately, freedom. Thank you for walking alongside me through the darkest valleys of my life and helping me see the light again. Because of your kindness and transformative messages, I am compelled to share this guide with others.

To you, the reader, my prayer is that the words and steps within these pages will offer you the same hope, clarity, and renewal that they provided me. May this book be a source of strength on your journey toward healing, restoration, and ultimately, freedom.

HOW THIS JOURNEY BEGAN

This book was born out of my personal story—a lifelong journey marked by heartbreak, healing, resilience, and rediscovery. There have been many situations in my life that felt like I had encountered hell on earth. While others were ***waiting to exhale***, I was ***waiting to exit hell***. For me, this wasn't just about enduring difficult moments, it was about surviving seasons of emotional, spiritual, and relational upheaval that left me questioning my worth, my purpose, and my ability to move forward.

As a single mother, I was determined to create the best life for my children possible. Anchored by my faith and the love I had for my family, I walked away from corporate America to pursue my dream of entrepreneurship. Yet, even with all that determination, I found myself in situations where compromise and confusion took over. These moments made me feel trapped in a cycle of pain, longing for the clarity and strength to break free. These are spaces I call "hell."

After years of healing from a divorce, I thought I was ready to embrace a new chapter. Then my mom transitioned. As I started to live again after an extended period of grief, I believed I had found someone who aligned with my values and shared my vision for life. But what began as hope and joy turned into a season of confusion, compromise, and heartbreak. In all these situations, I realized that I had given up or lost parts of myself and had to exit that particular hell in order to recover even some part of my God-breathed self.

Broken, repeatedly, wondering how I had gotten there and how I would ever get out. It was in those moments that I began to cry out to God for clarity, for direction, for a strategy to exit the hell that oftentimes I had created with my own choices. By His grace, I was reminded of my worth, my purpose, and His promises and with the support of friends, Scripture, and prayer, I began the process of healing and reclaiming my God-breathed identity rather than living miserably in the one forced on me by my environment and the people in it.

This journey was by no means linear. There were days of progress followed by days of setbacks; moments of breakthrough overshadowed by returns to old patterns of thinking and doing. Unlike before though, I now had a roadmap, a compass, and a companion for the journey. I was no longer waiting passively for deliverance; I was actively participating in my exit from hell.

The 31-day process outlined in these pages isn't a magic formula for instant healing, but rather a tested framework for intentional growth and restoration. Each day builds upon the previous one, helping you form habits that lead to healing, recognizing that true transformation takes time, perseverance, and divine intervention.

If you find yourself in your own version of hell right now—waiting, hurting, wondering if things will ever change—know that you're not alone. There is a way forward, and it begins with a single step, then another, and another. My prayer is that this guide will illuminate your path as you navigate your own journey from waiting to walking, from surviving to thriving, from hell to healing.

Your exit from hell begins now.

HOW *YOUR* JOURNEY BEGINS

"He brought me up also out of a horrible pit, out of the miry clay, and set my feet upon a rock, and established my goings." --Psalms 40:2

Welcome to your journey of healing, restoration, and recovery. This book was created to guide you through the emotional valleys of life and into the freedom and purpose God has destined for you. Whether you're overcoming a difficult relationship, releasing past regrets, or finding the courage to reclaim your identity, this guide will help you navigate the process with clarity and hope of exiting your hell.

Who Will Benefit from This Book?

This guide is for anyone feeling stuck in a season of emotional pain, uncertainty, or confusion. Perhaps you are recovering from a broken relationship, grappling with self-doubt, or simply feeling lost in the midst of life's challenges. Wherever you are on your journey, this book is designed to meet you there and walk with you toward freedom. It's for those ready to reclaim their identity, renew their purpose, and rediscover their worth.

How to Use This Book

This book is divided into three 10-day phases (with a bonus day at the end). Each day, you will encounter a Scripture Focus, a Reflection, an Exiting Hell Moment, Affirmation, and an Action Step or Journal Prompt. Take your time with each section. Begin your day by reading the Scripture and Reflection, allowing the words to speak to your heart. Review the Exiting Hell Moment and repeat the Affirmation throughout the day to reinforce your mindset. Finally, commit to completing the action step or journal prompt to actively engage in your healing process.

Be Intentional

This book is best experienced with intentionality. Set aside time each day to work through the content, even if it's only 15 minutes. Keep a dedicated journal for your reflections and prayers. Anytime you face an area of your life or a situation that causes you grief, pull this book back out and go through the process again—not just to revisit, but to grow through it. Whether you lose a relationship, experience significant grief, or encounter something that feels like you've entered your own personal hell, use this guide as a lifeline to help you regain clarity and restoration. The more you invest in this process, the greater the rewards will be.

Feeling Stuck

Life can feel like a never-ending waiting room. You know you're meant for more, you believe you have a greater purpose, but somehow, you're stuck in a cycle of pain, frustration, and delay. You're waiting for a break, a shift, a sign – something to show you that God has not forgotten about you.

If you have ever found yourself gasping for air under the weight of life's struggles, you're not alone. There are moments when life feels like a suffocating reality – one that holds you hostage in a place of fear, depression, regret, or confusion. You look around, and it seems that everyone else is exhaling, finding peace, moving forward – while you're just trying to survive and ultimately, to exit hell. We often think of hell as a final destination, a place reserved for the lost.

- What if hell isn't just an eternal punishment?

- What if hell is also the internal torment we experience here on earth – the emotional, spiritual, and mental battles that make us feel like we are drowning?

- What if hell is the toxic relationship that depletes your soul?

- What if hell is the financial struggle that leaves you hopeless?

- What if hell is the weight of unforgiveness, the pain of a loss, or the guilt of past mistakes?

- What if hell is living in a place where your dreams feel distant, and your faith feels weak?

Hell, in its many forms, tries to convince us that this is all there is, that this pit we are in is permanent. The devil is a liar.

The Truth About Your Waiting Season

You are not *waiting to exhale*.

You are *waiting to exit hell*.

And the exit is not just a destination; it's a series of decisions.

Psalm 40:2 says, "He brought me up also out of a horrible pit, out of the miry clay, and set my feet upon a rock, and established my goings."

This Scripture is a promise that no matter how deep the pit, God has made a way out. Your waiting season is about preparation, not about punishment. God is refining you, stretching you, and making room inside you for the person you are becoming as you align with His divine will and purpose for your life.

But let's be honest, waiting feels like warfare … because it is. When you're waiting on a breakthrough, the enemy will try to convince you that God has forgotten you. He will use distractions, discouragement, and even your own doubts to make you believe that the pit is permanent.

Our faith teaches us something different:

- Waiting is not the absence of movement. It is the alignment of divine timing.

- Waiting is not God ignoring you. It is God preparing you.

- Waiting is not wasted time; it is the space where your testimony is being built.

This book is designed to walk you through that process—to help you realize that your waiting season is actually the launch pad for your breakthrough.

A 31-Day Journey to Freedom

Over the next 31 days, we will journey together through the process of exiting the hells that have held us bound. Each devotional day will follow this format:

- **Scripture Focus** – This section provides a Bible verse or passage that serves as the foundation for the day's lesson. The verse is carefully selected to relate to the theme being explored and provides biblical grounding for the concepts discussed.

- **Reflection** – This section offers thoughtful commentary on the Scripture passage. It might include historical context, theological insights, or personal anecdotes that help you understand the deeper meaning of the verse. The reflection aims to inspire, encourage, and provide wisdom related to the day's theme.

- **Exiting Hell Moment** – This powerful section identifies negative thought patterns, harmful beliefs, or spiritual attacks that may have trapped you in emotional or spiritual distress. It presents biblical truth that directly counters these "lies" or destructive thoughts, helping you break free from harmful mindsets. Your first step out of hell is recognizing that you were never meant to stay there. The enemy wants you to believe that you are stuck, but faith declares that you are simply passing through.

- **Affirmation** – This section provides positive, faith-based declarations for you to declare your freedom. Speak out loud! These affirmations are written in first person ("I am...") and are designed to reinforce the truths learned, replacing negative self-talk with biblical promises and identity statements.

For example,

> *"I am not abandoned. God is with me in this season, and He is leading me out of my pit. I **inhale** hope, and I **exhale** fear. My steps are ordered, and my breakthrough is inevitable. My waiting is not wasted. My exit is coming. I am already walking in victory."*

- **Action Step/Journal Prompt** – This practical section moves you from knowing into doing. It provides a specific task, behavior change, prayer focus, or reflective question that helps you integrate the day's teaching into their daily lives, promoting lasting transformation. For instance,

    1. **Identify Your Hell** – Take a moment to be honest with yourself. What is the "hell" you've been living in? Is it fear? Financial struggles? Emotional pain? Write it down. Give it a name. It's time to confront it.

    2. **Recognize God's Presence** – Even in your darkest moments, God has been with you. Write down three moments when you know He showed up for you, even if it was in small ways.

    3. **Write Your Exit Declaration** – Declare in writing that you are coming out of this season stronger, wiser, and better. Start with: "I am exiting hell because…" and let your spirit speak.

    4. **Take a Small Faith Action** – Your exit begins with a single step. Maybe it's praying a bold prayer. Maybe it's cutting off a toxic relationship. Maybe it's seeking wise counsel. Whatever it is, commit to one step today.

This is not just another devotional. This is a battle plan.

You are not just waiting to *exhale*. You are waiting to *exit hell*. And by the time these 31 days are over, you will no longer be waiting. You will be walking into your next level, your breakthrough, your healing.

What to Expect as a Result

By the end of this journey, you can expect to feel lighter, freer, and more aligned with God's purpose for your life. You will gain clarity about your past, confidence in your present, and hope for your future. Through the daily challenges, you'll learn to let go of what no longer serves you, embrace your God-given identity, and walk boldly into the destiny He has prepared for you.

This is not a quick fix; it is a transformational process. Growth takes time, but with each day, you will take one step closer to emotional freedom and restoration. Together, let's declare that the constraints of the past no longer define you, and the torment of the present cannot hold you back.

TABLE OF CONTENTS

ACKNOWLEDGEMENT iii
HOW THIS JOURNEY BEGAN v
HOW *YOUR* JOURNEY BEGINS vii
A 31-Day Journey to Freedom xi

Phase 1: Initial Healing (Days 1-10) 1
   Day 1: In Your Anger, Do Not Sin 3
   Day 2: Break Free from Guilt 9
   Day 3: The Power of Forgiveness 13
   Day 4: Finding Peace in the Chaos 17
   Day 5: Strength for the Weary 23
   Day 6: God is not Finished with You 31
   Day 7: Choose Joy in the Midst of Pain 35
   Day 8: Don't Contemplate What Might Have Been 39
   Day 9: Finding Renewal When You're Weary 45
   Day 10: Cure Loneliness with Solitude 51

Phase 2: Inner Transformation (Days 11-20) 57
   Day 11: God Will Restore All You Lost 59
   Day 12: Trusting God's Timing 67
   Day 13: Embracing New Beginnings 73
   Day 14: Control Your Thinking 77
   Day 15: The Power of Your Words 83
   Day 16: God's Grace is Enough 87
   Day 17: Walking in Confidence 93
   Day 18: No Battle? No Victory 101
   Day 19: Breaking Chains and Moving Forward 107
   Day 20: Enter God's Rest 115

Phase 3: Empowerment and Moving Forward 125
   Day 21: Overcoming Fear with Faith 127

   Day 22: Stepping Into Your Purpose 133

   Day 23: The Power of Your Words - Creating Your Future 141

   Day 24: God Will Restore What You Lost - Participating in Restoration 149

   Day 25: Embracing Your New Identity 157

   Day 26: Building a Hopeful Future 163

   Day 27: Walking in Confidence - Living in Divine Assurance 169

   Day 28: Enter God's Rest – Establishing Sacred Rhythms 177

   Day 29: Breaking Chains and Moving Forward – Walking in Sustained Freedom 185

   Day 30: Celebrating Your Journey 193

   Day 31: From Surviving to Thriving - Your Journey Continues 199

Conclusion: Stepping Boldly into Your New Beginning 205

Affirmations by Phase 207

   Phase 1: Initial Healing (Days 1-10) 207

   Phase 2: Inner Transformation (Days 11-20) 211

   Phase 3: Empowerment and Future (Days 21-31) 215

Phase 1: Initial Healing
(Days 1-10)

Day 1: In Your Anger, Do Not Sin
Let it go ...

Scripture Focus

"In your anger, do not sin: Do not let the sun go down while you are still angry, and do not give the devil a foothold." — Ephesians 4:26-27 (NIV)

Reflection

Anger is one of the most powerful emotions we experience. It is raw, intense, and often overwhelming. It tells us that something deeply matters, but if left unchecked, it can become a destructive force in our lives. Today, we'll explore what it means to feel anger without being consumed by it. Often the root of our anger is bitterness. Someone said or did something that we just can't seem to get over. Those feelings fester and fester until there is a root of bitterness established. Ephesians 4:31 tells us clearly to "Let all bitterness, and wrath, and anger, and clamor, and evil speaking, be put away from you, with all malice." Bitterness is like drinking poison and expecting the other person to die. No. It is hurting you much more than it hurts them.

Imagine anger as a fire. When controlled, it can purify, refine, and even create positive change. But when allowed to run wild, it destroys everything in its path. Have you ever let anger dictate your actions or words, only to regret it later? Perhaps you lashed out at someone you love or allowed bitterness to seep into your thoughts, leaving you in a self-made prison. These moments can feel like hell on earth.

It's natural to look back at a period of your life that you devoted to a relationship and think about all that you lost in the process—enough to make you flat-out mad. The time you gave to someone who didn't deserve it. Time being the one thing that once you've spent it, you cannot get back.

What about everything else you gave? Trust, finances, energy, feelings, access, space, commitment, yourself. All things you cannot recover. All things that never were and never will be repaid or restored.

When these feelings of bitterness and resentment surface, it's important to remind yourself, daily, maybe even hourly, that moving on is what you need for your own personal growth and development, maybe even for your health. If you were to sit quietly and objectively, you know that being away from that situation is the best thing that could have happened to you. Entertaining thoughts of "getting back" at the other person only serves to wrap yourself back up with them. It's a form of holding on—keeping that person at the forefront of your mind, creating negative energy, and making them "what's important" again.

A Story of Transformation

There was a woman who struggled deeply with anger after losing her job unfairly. She felt betrayed by her employer and carried that resentment into every conversation and relationship. Her family noticed her short temper, and her friendships began to fade as people withdrew from her presence to avoid her bitterness. One day, during an intense argument with her husband, she realized her anger was costing her the relationships with the very people she cared about most. In that moment, she cried out to God, asking for help to release the burdens of her bitterness.

Over time, she began taking small steps to manage her anger. She started each day in prayer, asking God for peace and patience. She wrote her feelings in a journal rather than lashing out at those around her. Slowly but surely, as she did the work of healing internally, her relationships began to heal, and her heart felt lighter. She realized that letting go didn't mean the injustice was forgotten, but it meant she was no longer bound by it. She was taking her power back from the person that angered her.

To whom have you given your power? No one should have the ability to push your buttons nor cause you to behave in any way that you haven't already decided to behave. Anger, when unchecked, can lead to isolation, regret, and even more pain. But when surrendered to God, that same anger can be transformed into a catalyst for change and healing.

God's Perspective on Anger

Scripture reminds us: *"Do not be quickly provoked in your spirit, for anger resides in the lap of fools."* — Ecclesiastes 7:9 (NIV)

When someone has wronged you or hurt you deeply, God understands. He knows your heart and knows you would face these tribulations. And with that knowledge He said, "In your anger, do not sin." It may sound cliché, but God has your back. He created you and He knows you better than anyone else. And if God knows that in your anger you can NOT sin, then you can find that strength too.

But here's the good news: God doesn't call us to suppress our anger. Instead, He invites us to process it in a way that leads to peace, not destruction. Releasing anger is not about dismissing your feelings or pretending the hurt didn't happen. It's about finding freedom from the hold it has on your thoughts, your choices, and your future.

Notice I did not say find a way to get revenge. God tells us clearly that "vengeance is mine [His], and recompense, for the time when their foot shall slip; for the day of their calamity is at hand, and their doom comes swiftly (Deut. 32:35)." God will handle it. If we try to handle it, whatever happens will be our reward. Let go and let God be God.

When Anger Threatens to Overtake You

What do you do when these feelings creep up, when anger, resentment, pain, and the desire for revenge are hard to manage?

1. Read aloud Ephesians 4:25-27 (NIV): *"Therefore each of you must put off falsehood and speak truthfully to your neighbor, for we are all members of one body. 'In your anger do not sin': Do not let the sun go down while you are still angry, and do not give the devil a foothold."*

2. Pray for the healing and peace only God can provide.

3. Write in your journal all that you are thankful and grateful for and think on those things. (Philippians 4:8)

4. Remember: You wanted and needed to be out anyway.

Think about a time when your anger controlled you. How did it impact your relationships, your peace, or your sense of self? Now imagine what it would feel like to surrender that anger to God, trusting Him to fight the battles you can't.

This isn't easy. But carrying the weight of resentment is far harder. God calls us to let go of anger, not because the other person deserves forgiveness, but because *you* deserve peace. Choose to release the anger, one day, one hour, one minute, even one second at a time.

Exiting Hell Moment

Anger can feel like a tether keeping you in emotional torment. Today, commit to cutting that cord. You may even want to draw a picture of you in your journal, cutting the cord with the person or situation that hurt you.

Picture yourself standing at the gates of hell, refusing to step inside, instead choosing the peace God offers. Every time you release anger, you are stepping further away from the fire and closer to the freedom of exhaling and resting in God's peace.

Affirmation

I release anger and embrace peace. My future is too important to be tied to the past. I stand liberated from the chains of resentment that once held me captive, choosing instead to walk in the freedom of forgiveness and the boundless possibilities that await me in God's perfect plan for my life.

Action Step/Journal Prompt

Write a letter to the person or situation that caused your anger. Let it all out on paper. Then, take a moment to pray over it, asking God to help you let go of the anger related to the situation. When you're ready, destroy the letter as a symbolic act of release. Tear it up, flush it down the toilet or otherwise destroy it. Reflect in your journal on how this process made you feel.

Day 2: Breaking Free from Guilt

Scripture Focus

"Therefore, there is now no condemnation to them which are in Christ Jesus, who walk not after the flesh, but after the Spirit."— Romans 8:1

Reflection

Guilt can be one of the heaviest burdens you will ever carry. It whispers lies about your worth and keeps you chained to past mistakes. It causes you to replay your errors over and over, wondering if there's any way to make things right. Guilt, as heavy as it is, is not meant to be a life sentence. God's grace declares something entirely different: you are forgiven. His grace is sufficient for you.

There was a man who made a series of poor decisions that damaged his family and hurt those he loved. He carried the weight of that guilt for years, believing he didn't deserve forgiveness. Each morning, he woke up feeling unworthy and ashamed. His guilt affected every aspect of his life, his relationships, his work, and even his health. One day, he stumbled upon Romans 8:1: "Therefore, there is now no condemnation for those who are in Christ Jesus." For the first time, he realized that guilt based on past mistakes did not define him. He began the process of releasing his guilt to God. He asked for forgiveness and worked to make amends where possible. As he embraced God's grace, he felt a freedom he hadn't known in years.

The Enemy's Tool vs. God's Truth

Guilt is a tool the enemy uses to keep you stuck, to make you believe that you are beyond redemption and unworthy of God's unmerited grace.

God's Word tells us that there is no condemnation for those in Christ. Think about that—no condemnation. Not "some," not "a little," but none. You are not your mistake. You are not the sum of your failures. You are a child of God, redeemed by His grace and restored through His love.

Consider King David. After his grievous sins of adultery and murder, David was consumed by guilt. In Psalm 51, he poured out his heart to God, saying, "Create in me a clean heart, O God, and renew a steadfast spirit within me" (Psalm 51:10). David didn't hide his guilt; he brought it to God. And what did God do? He forgave David and restored him. Not only that, David has the distinction of being known as a "man after God's own heart (Acts 13:22)." Even with all he did. David's story reminds us that no sin, nor any frequency of sin, is too great for God's grace. The same God who forgave David forgives you today. All we have to do is ask and receive.

The Process of Release

Releasing guilt starts with accepting God's forgiveness. It's not about earning your way back into His favor—it's about receiving the gift of grace that Jesus has already provided. We cannot earn God's forgiveness, we cannot be sorry enough, good enough, clean enough, nothing enough, to merit God's forgiveness. It's only through His grace that we are forgiven. Can you imagine if we could work our way into God's grace and blessings? How arrogant would we be thinking that somehow, we had a lock on God's grace and favor?

Guilt not only weighs you down but also distorts how you see yourself and others. It can make you overly critical, fearful of making new mistakes, or hesitant to pursue the life God has for you. But when you let go of guilt, you make room for healing, growth, and restoration. Forgiveness doesn't mean you forget your mistakes; it means you no longer let them control you. Instead, you learn from them and move forward with wisdom and grace.

Practical Steps Forward

Practical steps can help you release guilt:

1. Start by confessing your sins to God. Be honest and specific, trusting that He already knows your heart.

2. Accept His forgiveness. This step might take time—it's not always easy to forgive yourself—but remember that if God has forgiven you, you have no right to hold onto guilt.

3. If possible, seek to make amends with those you've wronged. A heartfelt apology can be a powerful step toward reconciliation and healing.

Reflect on how guilt has held you back. Has it stopped you from pursuing opportunities, building relationships, or fully embracing God's love? Now imagine what your life could look like without that weight. What doors might open? What open doors might you need to walk through? What peace might fill your heart? Releasing guilt isn't just about finding relief; it's about stepping into the freedom and purpose God has for you.

Imagine this: You're standing at the edge of a vast ocean, the waves gently lapping at your feet. Each wave represents God's grace, washing over you and carrying away the weight of guilt. As the water recedes, you feel lighter, freer, and more at peace. This is the power of God's forgiveness—it doesn't just cover your mistakes; it removes them entirely, leaving you renewed and restored. Thank you, Lord!

Exiting Hell Moment

Guilt can feel like its own hell, chaining you to the past. Today, choose to break free. Confess your mistakes to God, and trust that His forgiveness is real. **Inhale** grace, **exhale** guilt. This is another great exchange that we have access through by the death, burial and resurrection of our Lord and Savior Jesus Christ.

Affirmation

I am completely forgiven, gloriously redeemed, and radiantly free in Christ, walking in the fullness of grace that has broken every chain and washed away every stain of my past. The blood of Jesus has transformed me from a prisoner of shame into a beloved child of God, empowered by His Spirit to live victoriously today and face tomorrow with unshakable confidence in His unfailing promises.

Action Step/Journal Prompt

Write a letter to God, confessing anything you feel guilty about. Then, write a second letter to yourself, reminding yourself of God's forgiveness and grace. Reflect on how it feels to let go of guilt.

Picture yourself standing with a heavy backpack filled with stones, each one representing a mistake or regret. Now imagine Jesus standing before you, holding out His hands. He says, "Give it to Me." As you hand Him the backpack, He takes it, and suddenly, you feel lighter. That's what forgiveness does, it lifts the burden of guilt and replaces it with peace. Some of us need to get a backpack, fill it with rocks that we have written the things that we regret and the mistakes that we made on them. You will put down those rocks with a quickness – assuming you could ever really pick them up.

Day 3: The Power of Forgiveness

Scripture Focus

"Bear with each other and forgive one another if any of you has a grievance against someone. Forgive as the Lord forgave you." — Colossians 3:13 (NIV)

Reflection

Forgiveness is one of the most powerful acts of faith. It's not about excusing the hurt but about releasing its hold on you. As we stated on Day 1, holding on to bitterness is like drinking poison and expecting the other person to suffer. The reality is that unforgiveness doesn't imprison the offender—it imprisons you. Forgiveness is how you set yourself free.

Think about Joseph, the beloved son of Jacob, who was betrayed by his own brothers, thrown into a pit, and sold into slavery. He suffered injustice upon injustice, from being falsely accused to being forgotten in prison. If anyone had a reason to hold onto resentment, it was Joseph. Yet, when he was finally in a position of power and had the chance to retaliate, he chose to forgive. "You intended to harm me, but God intended it for good to accomplish what is now being done, the saving of many lives." Genesis 50:20 (NIV). His act of forgiveness didn't just restore his family, it positioned him for God's greater plan.

The Freedom of Letting Go

There is a woman I know that carried deep resentment toward her father for abandoning her as a child. Somewhere around her 11th birthday, he disappeared and only interacted with her when there was trouble. Her un forgiveness shaped every aspect of her life. As a teen, she looked for love in the arms of any male that would give her attention. What she really wanted began to be what she really repelled. She built walls in relationships, mistrusted others, and lived with a guarded heart. One day, she realized that her anger wasn't punishing her father—it was punishing her. She chose to let go, not for his sake, but for hers. As she forgave, she felt a weight lifted. She found peace she had never known before, all because she chose to release the chains of bitterness. As a bonus, she was finally free to obey the Bible and honor her father the way we are commanded. What an incredible blessing.

How many times have you been hurt and once you get past the unforgiveness, you arrive in a place where you can see objectively and realize that what happened was exactly what needed to happen to position you where God wanted you?

Forgiveness doesn't mean forgetting or pretending the hurt never happened. It means choosing not to let that hurt define you. When Jesus was on the cross, He prayed, "Father, forgive them, for they do not know what they are doing." Luke 23:34 (NIV) He demonstrated that forgiveness is a choice, a supernatural act of love and faith. They didn't have to beg or plead, cry or pray, fast or lay hands on the sick. They only had to receive what Jesus was offering. We know this because one of the criminals hanging alongside Jesus simply asked to be remembered and Jesus agreed that he would be with him in paradise. It's not our works, it's our humility.

Unforgiveness creates a cycle of pain. Forgiveness breaks that cycle. It allows you to step into healing and restoration. More importantly, it allows you to be forgiven. The enemy wants you to stay trapped in anger and resentment because it keeps you from walking in the freedom of forgiveness. God calls you to something higher—to release the burden and walk in love.

Practical Steps Toward Forgiveness

1. **Acknowledge the Hurt** – Denying the pain won't heal it. Be honest with yourself about what happened and how it affected you.

2. **Pray for Strength** – Forgiveness isn't easy, but God can empower you to do it.

3. **Decide to Release It** – Forgiveness is not a feeling; it's a choice. You may not feel ready, but choosing to forgive begins the healing process.

4. **Pray for the Person that Hurt You** – Most often, this is easier said than done. When you pray for the one who hurt you, your heart begins to soften though.

5. **Give Yourself Grace** – Forgiveness is often a process, not a one-time event. It may take deciding a thousand times to forgive before you start to feel like it. Keep surrendering it to God until you feel free.

6. **Forgive Yourself** – Often we are our own worst enemy. Allow yourself to operate in forgiveness for yourself.

A Journey to Freedom

Consider a woman who was betrayed by a close friend. The pain was deep, and the anger was consuming. For years, she held onto that bitterness, refusing to forgive. But bitterness began to seep into other areas of her life, affecting her joy and relationships. One day, she read Colossians 3:13 and realized forgiveness wasn't about letting the friend off the hook; it was about freeing herself.

She prayed for the strength to forgive, and over time, she felt the chains of bitterness fall away. While forgiveness didn't erase the pain, it did allow her to move forward with peace.

Exiting Hell Moment

Unforgiveness is a personal hell that traps you in the past. Today, take a step toward freedom by choosing to forgive. *Exhale* resentment and *inhale* God's peace.

Remember that backpack from Day 2? Imagine you've been carrying it filled with bricks labeled "resentment," "anger," and "hurt." Each step you take feels harder, weighed down by the past. Now, picture Jesus standing before you with open arms. He says, "Give it to Me." You hesitate, but then you release the backpack. Suddenly, you feel lighter, freer. That's what forgiveness does— it lifts the burden and replaces it with peace.

Affirmation

I release bitterness and choose forgiveness, breaking free from the prison of resentment that once held my heart captive and poisoned my spirit. I am free to walk in the light of grace, unburdened by the weight of past hurts, empowered to embrace each new day with a heart cleansed by mercy and hope to the abundant joy that flows from choosing love over anger.

Action Step/Journal Prompt

Who is it that you need to forgive? Write down their name(s). Pray for them, asking God to bless them. You may have to first pray for the power to forgive. Make the decision to forgive and watch forgiveness wash over you. Reflect on how this act of forgiveness feels and how it begins to lighten your heart.

Day 4: Finding Peace in the Chaos

Scripture Focus

"Peace, I leave with you; my peace I give you. I do not give to you as the world gives. Do not let your hearts be troubled and do not be afraid."—John 14:27 (NIV)

Reflection

Life is unpredictable, and chaos seems to be all around us. In the midst of stress, uncertainty, and disappointment, peace can feel like an impossible dream. But Jesus offers us a peace that transcends circumstances—a peace that is not dependent on what is happening around us but rooted in who is within us.

The world defines peace as the absence of conflict. The peace of God exists even in the midst of conflict, in the middle of the storm. When the disciples were caught in a violent storm at sea, they panicked while Jesus slept peacefully. When they woke Him in fear, He simply spoke, "Peace, be still," and the wind and waves obeyed. (Mark 4:39) The same Jesus who calmed that storm is with you now and by His Spirit, He's empowered you to speak to the storm and consequently, speak peace into your life and into the lives of those around you.

God's Peace vs. Worldly Peace

True peace is not the absence of problems, but the presence of God in the midst of them. We often believe that if our circumstances change, then we would finally have peace. God's peace is different. It allows us to remain steady and unshaken, even when the world around us is in turmoil.

Think about Daniel in the lion's den. Daniel knew long before he faced the lions that God was a lion tamer. He had experienced God's salvation before. He faced an unjust punishment, surrounded by danger. Yet he did not panic. He remained calm because he trusted God completely. And what happened? God shut the mouths of the lions. Peace is not about controlling everything—it's about trusting the One who is in control.

Biblical Examples of Peace Amid Chaos

Throughout Scripture, we see powerful examples of individuals who found peace in chaotic circumstances.

> **Paul and Silas** were beaten and thrown into prison, their bodies bruised and their future uncertain. What was their response? Acts 16:25 tells us they were praying and singing hymns to God at midnight. Their peace wasn't dependent on freedom or comfort but on their unwavering faith in God's goodness. Their praise in prison led to an earthquake that broke their chains and opened the prison doors—a powerful reminder that praise often precedes breakthrough. Let me say that another way, praise is a weapon to bring breakthrough into any situation.

> **Queen Esther** faced a seemingly impossible situation. Her people were marked for destruction, and approaching the king uninvited could mean death for her. In this crisis, she requested prayer and fasting, centered herself in God's presence, and found the courage to say, "If I perish, I perish." (Esther 4:16) Her peace came from surrendering the outcome to God, which ultimately led to the salvation of her people.

> **King David** experienced chaos throughout his life—being hunted by Saul, facing rebellion from his own son, enduring the consequences of his mistakes. Yet he wrote in Psalm 23:2, "He leads me beside quiet waters, he refreshes my soul." David knew that even in life's valleys, God's peace was available. This wasn't a denial of reality but a deeper awareness of God's presence within it.

The Physiology of Peace

When we're anxious or stressed, our bodies release cortisol and adrenaline, preparing us for "fight or flight." Our heart rate increases, our breathing becomes shallow, and our minds race with worst-case scenarios. This physical response to chaos can leave us exhausted and overwhelmed.

But when we intentionally seek God's peace, something remarkable happens physiologically. Deep breathing and prayer can activate our parasympathetic nervous system, slowing our heart rate and reducing stress hormones. Meditating on Scripture can literally rewire neural pathways, creating new thought patterns that lead to peace rather than panic.

Philippians 4:6-7 (NIV) gives us the spiritual prescription for anxiety: "Do not be anxious about anything, but in every situation, by prayer and petition, with thanksgiving, present your requests to God. And the peace of God, which transcends all understanding, will guard your hearts and your minds in Christ Jesus." This isn't just spiritual advice; it's a practical pathway to peace that affects both body and soul.

Practical Steps to Finding Peace

When you feel like your life is spinning out of control, here's how you can anchor yourself in God's peace:

1. **Pray** – In moments of stress, take a deep breath and turn to God in prayer. Once you have prayed, release your worries to Him and enter a space of praising Him for the answers. Make prayer your first response, not your last resort.

2. **Trust His Control** – Remind yourself that God is sovereign. He is not surprised by your situation and already has a plan for your good. When you can't trace His hand, trust His heart.

3. **Focus on His Promises** – Meditate on Scriptures that affirm His peace and faithfulness. Write them on cards, set them as phone reminders, speak them aloud when anxiety rises.

4. **Guard Your Mind** – Fill your thoughts with things that bring peace, not stress. Limit negativity and focus on gratitude. As Philippians 4:8 instructs, think about whatever is true, noble, right, pure, lovely, admirable, excellent, or praiseworthy.

5. **Rest in His Presence** – Take time to be still before God. Worship, journal, or sit in silence, allowing Him to calm your spirit. Sometimes the most spiritual thing you can do is simply rest.

When Peace Feels Impossible

Perhaps you're thinking, "This sounds nice, but my situation is too far gone for peace." Maybe you're facing a devastating medical diagnosis, a broken relationship, financial ruin, or the loss of a loved one. How do you find peace when your world is truly falling apart?

First, know that it's okay to acknowledge your pain. Jesus Himself wept at Lazarus's tomb and sweat drops of blood in Gethsemane. Again, peace doesn't mean denying reality—it means finding God in the midst of it.

Second, remember that peace often comes in moments, not seasons. Even in your darkest hour, God offers pockets of His presence—brief respites where His peace breaks through. Look for these moments and cherish them.

Third, lean on the body of Christ. Sometimes we find peace through the prayers, presence, and practical support of other believers who hold hope for us when we cannot hold it for ourselves.

Finally, remember that some forms of chaos are actually part of God's redemptive work. Just as a surgeon must create a wound to heal a deeper one, God may allow disruption to bring deeper peace and healing. Trust His process, even when it's painful.

Peace as a Witness

When you maintain peace in the midst of chaos, it becomes a powerful testimony to others. People notice when you respond differently to stress, disappointment, and fear. Your peace becomes a window through which others can glimpse the God you serve.

Consider the early Christians who faced persecution with such supernatural peace that their Roman executioners sometimes converted on the spot. Or think of modern believers in war-torn countries who minister with joy despite constant danger. This kind of peace isn't just for your benefit—it's a light that draws others to Christ.

Jesus said, "Blessed are the peacemakers," (Matthew 5:9) suggesting that we're not just recipients of peace but carriers of it. As you receive God's peace, look for opportunities to extend it to others—through a calm word in a heated moment, a reassuring presence in someone else's storm, or intercession for those in turmoil.

Finding the Eye of the Storm

Imagine this: You are standing in the middle of a storm, the wind howling, rain pouring, and chaos swirling around you. But in the center of it all, there is a still, quiet space where God's presence dwells. As you step into that space, the storm loses its power over you. You may not control the storm, but you are not controlled by it either. That is the peace of God.

Meteorologists tell us that in the eye of a hurricane—the center of the most violent storm—there is perfect calm. The winds may rage at 150 miles per hour around it, but in that central space, the skies are clear and the air is still. What a perfect picture of God's peace! The circumstances haven't changed, but in that sacred space of God's presence, you can experience calm amid the chaos.

Exiting Hell Moment

When chaos feels overwhelming, the enemy wants you to believe there is no way out. But God has already made a way. Today, choose to receive His peace. **Exhale** anxiety and **inhale** divine calm. Step out of the hellish prison of panic and into the freedom of faith. As you do, you'll discover that peace isn't just the absence of chaos—it's the presence of Christ in the midst of it.

Affirmation

I receive God's perfect peace that flows like a river through every corner of my soul, washing away all anxiety and filling me with divine tranquility that the world cannot give or take away. My heart is at peace and I am not afraid, for I am securely held in the loving hands of my Heavenly Father who commands the wind and waves and whose powerful presence surrounds me with an unshakable calm even in life's fiercest storms.

Action Step/Journal Prompt

Write down three situations in your life that are causing you stress. Next to each, write a truth from God's Word about His peace. Speak these truths over your life daily. Then, create a "peace practice" - a specific routine (prayer, Scripture reading, worship, or quiet reflection) that you commit to follow the next time chaos threatens to overwhelm you.

Day 5: Strength for the Weary

Scripture Focus

"But those who hope in the Lord will renew their strength. They will soar on wings like eagles; they will run and not grow weary; they will walk and not be faint." — Isaiah 40:31

Reflection

There are days when exhaustion takes over—mentally, emotionally, physically, and spiritually. You try to keep going, but the weight of life feels too heavy. In these moments, you need to remember that your strength does not come from within; it comes from God.

> *"You are so strong. You don't even realize your own power. With your mind and heart in the right place and God at the helm, you are unstoppable! If you don't know, I know." ~signed, your friend.*

Elijah was a mighty prophet, but he even experienced deep exhaustion. After a great victory against the prophets of Baal, he found himself running for his life, drained and discouraged. He collapsed under a tree and prayed to die. But God met him there, providing food, rest, and reassurance (1 Kings 19:4-8). God didn't criticize Elijah for being weary—He strengthened him for the journey ahead.

Our Weakness Reveals God's Strength

"I just can't do it." "It's just too much." Have you ever spoken those words when facing a situation that seems too great? Perhaps you've been offered a promotion at work but are afraid you're not skilled enough. You may have been asked to teach a Sunday School class but fear you don't know the Bible well enough. God may have put it on your heart to write, and release for public scrutiny, a book, but the voice that clamors for your attention says that you'll fail. Often the thing that God lays out for us to do is bigger than we are and will somehow force our dependence on Him.

The good news is that it isn't at all about our goodness, strength, or wisdom. In fact, the opposite is true. God chooses those who are inadequate in and of themselves so that the ultimate glory goes to Him. Said differently, when we finally come to the end of ourselves and relinquish control, the will of God will take over and He will get all of the glory.

"Because the foolishness of God is wiser than men, and the weakness of God is stronger than men. For you see your calling, brethren, that not many wise according to the flesh, not many mighty, not many nobles are called. But God has chosen the foolish things of the world to put to shame the wise, and God has chosen the weak things of the world to put to shame the things which are mighty; and the base things of the world and the things which are despised God has chosen, and the things which are not, to bring to nothing the things that are. That no flesh should glory in His presence." (1 Corinthians 1:25-29, NKJV)

When we serve out of our weakness and God's strength, it is obvious to everyone that the power of Holy Spirit, not human strength or wisdom, has accomplished remarkable things.

The Misunderstanding of Strength

We often equate strength with productivity, pushing ourselves to keep going even when our souls are depleted. True strength is found in surrender—knowing when to rest and allow God to renew us. Sometimes, the bravest thing you can do is admit you need help and lean on God for the strength to continue.

Isaiah 40:31 reminds us that those who hope in the Lord will renew their strength. This renewal is not just about physical energy but about restoring our hearts, minds, and spirits. God promises to lift us up, to help us soar, even when we feel grounded by life's burdens.

Types of Weariness We Face

Weariness comes in many forms, and often we experience multiple types simultaneously:

1. **Physical Weariness** - Our bodies become exhausted from overwork, lack of sleep, illness, or the demands of daily life. When we're physically tired, everything else feels more difficult.

2. **Emotional Weariness** - The weight of grief, anxiety, disappointment, or conflict can drain our emotional reserves, leaving us feeling empty and overwhelmed.

3. **Mental Weariness** - Constant decision-making, problem-solving, and information overload can lead to mental fatigue, making it difficult to think clearly or focus.

4. **Spiritual Weariness** - Sometimes our faith feels dry, our prayers seem unanswered, and God feels distant. This spiritual exhaustion can be the most challenging to overcome.

No matter which type of weariness you're experiencing, God offers renewal and strength for each area of need.

Biblical Examples of Renewed Strength

Moses grew weary leading the Israelites through the wilderness. During a battle with the Amalekites, he had to keep his hands raised for Israel to prevail. When he couldn't hold them up any longer, Aaron and Hur supported his arms until victory was secured (Exodus 17:8-13). This illustrates how God will use the support of others to bring strength to us.

David frequently wrote about his exhaustion and how God renewed him. In Psalm 23, he describes God leading him beside quiet waters and restoring his soul. In Psalm 18:1-2, he calls God his strength and fortress. Even when fleeing from enemies or facing enormous challenges, David found that God's strength was sufficient.

Paul described a "thorn in the flesh" that tormented him. When he prayed for its removal, God answered, "My grace is sufficient for you, for my power is made perfect in weakness." 2 Corinthians 12:9 (NIV). Paul learned to boast in his weaknesses so that Christ's power could rest on him.

Dependence on God

Each day as you go about your business, acknowledge that in your own strength, you can't do it. Only God can. Put your dependence completely in God knowing that in your weakness, He is made strong. Throw yourself into the arms of Jesus and ask Him to carry you as you do the work, He has called you to do.

As you begin to see success, don't forget that it is God who strengthens you, provides the ability for you to do the work, gives you favor, and opens doors. It isn't about you, but about the God who deserves all the honor and glory. He is the One who should be acknowledged in the midst of "your" success.

The Paradox of Strength Through Rest

In our busy world, resting often feels like weakness or laziness. God's economy works differently. Sometimes the most productive thing you can do is rest. Jesus Himself withdrew regularly to pray and rest (Luke 5:16), modeling the rhythm of work and renewal that God designed us to follow.

Rest isn't just about sleeping more, although that's important. It's about:

- **Sabbath**: Setting aside regular time to cease productivity and simply be in God's presence

- **Solitude**: Finding quiet spaces to hear God's voice amid the noise

- **Simplicity**: Removing unnecessary burdens and commitments

- **Surrender**: Letting go of what you can't control and trusting God with the outcomes

In Matthew 11:28-30, when Jesus invited the weary to come to Him for rest, He wasn't offering a temporary break but a new way of living—one where His strength becomes ours as we learn to carry His light yoke. We'll talk about this more on another day.

How to Receive God's Strength

Here's how to receive God's strength in seasons of weariness:

1. **Acknowledge Your Need** – Don't push through on your own. Admit when you are struggling and ask God for help. Vulnerability before God is the beginning of renewal.

2. **Pause and Recharge** – Spiritual and physical rest are essential. Create margins in your life—spaces where you can breathe and hear God's voice.

3. **Renew Your Mind** – Replace exhaustion-driven negative thoughts with God's promises of strength. Memorize verses like Isaiah 40:31, Philippians 4:13, or 2 Corinthians 12:9 to counteract the lies that weariness whispers.

4. **Lean on Community** – Let others support you in prayer and encouragement. Like Moses needed Aaron and Hur,

sometimes God's strength comes through the hands and hearts of fellow believers.

5. **Take One Step at a Time** – You don't have to have it all figured out. Trust God with each small step forward. Remember that God's strength is often given just for today's journey, not tomorrow's mountains.

The Power of Hope

Notice that Isaiah 40:31 begins with "those who hope in the Lord." Hope is the fuel that powers our renewal. When we lose hope, weariness takes over completely. But biblical hope isn't wishful thinking, it's a confident expectation based on God's character and promises.

Cultivating hope means fixing our eyes, not on our circumstances, but on the God who transcends them. It means remembering His faithfulness in the past and trusting His goodness for the future. As hope grows, so does our capacity to receive His strength.

A Fresh Perspective

Imagine this: You are running a marathon, and your legs feel like they will give out at any moment. Suddenly, you see a friend standing on the sidelines with a cup of water, cheering you on. You take the water, drink deeply, and feel a renewed sense of strength to continue. That friend is God, and His strength is available to you every single day.

When you feel weary, remember that God doesn't just give strength—He is strength. He doesn't just offer renewal—He is the source of all life and energy. And He hasn't called you to deplete yourself in His service but to serve from the overflow of His power working through you.

Exiting Hell Moment

Weariness can feel like a prison, draining your hope. Today, receive God's strength. Let Him carry what is too heavy for you. ***Inhale*** *His power and* ***exhale*** *His power.*

When you're too tired to even pray, remember that Holy Spirit intercedes for you with "groans that words cannot express" (Romans 8:26). You don't have to find the words or summon the energy—simply turn your heart toward the One who promises to renew your strength. Step out of the hell of exhaustion and into the freedom of dependence on God's unlimited power.

Affirmation

The Lord renews my strength with divine power that infuses every fiber of my being, transforming my weakness into supernatural ability and my fatigue into heavenly energy that never depletes. I will soar on wings like eagles above life's challenges, run the race set before me without growing weary, and walk forward in unwavering faith that carries me through every valley and mountaintop with the steadfast assurance that my God goes before me, behind me, and beside me in every step of my journey.

Action Step/Journal Prompt

Write about an area in your life where you feel weary. Ask God to strengthen you, then list three practical ways you can allow Him to renew you today. Consider what you need to surrender or set aside to make space for His renewal in your life.

Day 6: God is not Finished with You ...
You Are Still Here

Scripture Focus

"I know your deeds, that you are neither cold nor hot. I wish you were either one or the other! So, because you are lukewarm—neither hot nor cold—I am about to spit you out of my mouth." — Revelation 3:15-16 (NIV)

Reflection

Sometimes, the simple truth that you are still alive can be a revelation. When life feels like an uphill battle and you've been through what seems like endless trials, you may find yourself asking, "Why am I still here?" The answer is clear: God is not finished with you yet.

You are alive because God is not finished with you; your story is not over. Your story didn't end with them, and God has so much more for you. THANK GOD that your story didn't end there. Where would you have ended up? What would you have compromised?

Let's consider the story of Joseph. Sold into slavery by his own brothers, falsely accused, and thrown into prison, Joseph endured years of hardship. Yet, through it all, he remained faithful, trusting in God's plan for his life. Eventually, he rose to a position of great influence in Egypt, saving many lives during a famine. His survival through betrayal, injustice, and suffering wasn't just endurance—it was preparation for his God-ordained purpose. Like Joseph, your survival is not just about enduring; it's about stepping into the life God has prepared for you.

The Danger of Compromise

Compromise is a deadly sin. A friend of mine was involved in a relationship with a man that she knew was a plant from the enemy. Not that he was mean or abusive, he just didn't honor her. She tried everything to make that relationship work and it didn't. She couldn't understand why things were always going wrong for her both in and out of the relationship. She didn't know why she was so constantly anxious and worried. Her insides were in shambles, but from the outside, she appeared happy and content. When she cried to me for advice, God placed it in my heart to tell her one thing: "You know why things aren't going right." It sounded callous to me, I second-guessed myself, but when I told her what I heard in my spirit, the tears began to fall.

When you are in a compromised state, your relationship with God suffers severely. When you know what you are supposed to do and you don't, you open yourself up for the enemy to attack you in your mind, body, and in life, causing a domino effect that will manifest in every area of your life. Christ says He is The Way, the truth, and the life, and no one goes to the Father except through Him.

Have you ever had a disagreement with someone and wanted a third party to tell him/her that they are WRONG? How frustrating is it to have that third party agree with both sides? They are 'lukewarm' to the situation; they refuse to choose a side. At the end of the conversation, nothing is decided, and you are at the same place you started. Don't be a lukewarm Christian, stand firm in your belief, don't compromise for anyone, and be assured that you will be rewarded for your faithfulness.

Embracing Your God-Given Life

Each breath you take is proof that your story isn't over. Think about a moment in your life when you thought you wouldn't make it—when the pain, grief, or challenges seemed insurmountable. Yet, here you are, still standing. That's no accident—it's God's grace. He sees you, loves you, and has a plan for you. Your scars are not signs of weakness but evidence of battles won and lessons learned. They remind you of God's faithfulness and the strength He has given you to overcome.

Yes, you may feel weary, but weariness is an opportunity to lean into God's strength. Consider these words from Isaiah 40:31 (NIV): "But those who hope in the Lord will renew their strength. They will soar on wings like eagles; they will run and not grow weary; they will walk and not be faint." God promises to renew your strength as you trust in Him. Every day you wake up, you have the chance to start again, to walk one step further from the fires of hell and closer to the abundant life God promises.

Survival is more than just existing—it's an opportunity to grow, to learn, and to become the person God created you to be. Your life has meaning and purpose, even in the midst of trials. Like gold refined in fire, you are being shaped and strengthened through the challenges you face.

Decide today what side you will stand on and stay there!

Exiting Hell Moment

Hell tells you that your struggles define you and that your pain is permanent. But God says otherwise. Today, reflect on the fact that being alive is a gift. Like Joseph, who stepped out of prison into his purpose, each moment you choose to embrace hope, you are actively exiting the grip of despair. Take a deep breath and ***inhale*** life and ***exhale*** compromise. You are alive, and that is a victory worth celebrating.

Affirmation

I am alive and thriving because God is not finished with me yet, His divine purpose for my life unfolding with perfect timing and wisdom far beyond my limited understanding. Each breath I take declares His ongoing masterpiece within me, transforming my weaknesses into strengths, my trials into testimony, and my broken places into channels for His glory to shine through with breathtaking brilliance that testifies to His unfailing faithfulness and limitless love.

Action Step/Journal Prompt

Write a list of all the things you've survived that once seemed impossible. Next to each one, jot down how God carried you through it. Reflect on what this says about His faithfulness and His plans for your future. Use this as your list of touchstones. If He did it before, He'll do it again. Same God right now, same God back then.

Day 7: Choose Joy in the Midst of Pain

Scripture Focus

"The joy of the Lord is your strength." — Nehemiah 8:10

Reflection

Men and women tend to process broken relationships differently. For a woman, it's often the crashing and burning of her world. For a man, it's a crashing and burning in one single area of their lives. Men are exceptionally good at compartmentalizing. The processing of the pain is what gets us most often.

"The LORD is my rock, and my fortress and my deliverer; my God is my strength, in whom I will trust; my buckler, and the horn of my salvation, and my high tower." – Psalms 18:2

Joy might feel out of reach when life is hard. It's not. Joy isn't dependent on circumstances—it's rooted in knowing who God is and trusting Him through the process. Joy is a choice, an act of defiance against despair, and a declaration that pain won't have the final say in your life.

Different Ways of Processing Pain

Men usually process a breakup differently than women. For men, it is often a blow to the ego. There are no girlfriends to cry to, no pints of ice cream and sad movies that help process the negative emotions. There's just a man trying to 'fix' his painful feelings. Fixing it can include other women, alcohol, ignoring their feelings, and completely denying the breakup for a time. Men by nature are pain carriers; they will 'push down,' try to ignore and cover up their pain, which inevitably leads to depression and stress. The new woman/car/wardrobe can never completely heal the pain carrier.

For that reason, men who are divorced are twice as likely as divorced women to die prematurely. The more hurt a man is behind his breakup, the quicker he will try to move on to mask the hurt. In order to heal, you have to decide to feel the pain, yes even to embrace the pain. It hurts. When it crosses your mind, know that yes, you are sad, yes it hurts. But tomorrow won't hurt like today; each day will get easier.

You have two options. You can be a

- **Pain Carrier** that gets hurt and lives a dark and heavy life covered by deep negative thoughts, depression, and stress, or a
- **Pain Processor** that gets hurt, processes the event, and lives a life of contentment, joy, and productivity.

It's your choice.

Learning from Biblical Examples

One of the most prominent figures in the Bible, Paul, while imprisoned, wrote some of the most uplifting letters filled with joy and hope, including his letter to the Philippians. Paul's circumstances were dire—he was chained, restricted, and uncertain about his future. Yet, he declared, "Rejoice in the Lord always: and again I say rejoice." (Philippians 4:4). Paul's joy wasn't tied to his physical freedom but to his relationship with Christ. He knew that joy wasn't the absence of suffering but the presence of God in the midst of our suffering. Knowing you're not alone and have never been alone.

Now, think about your own life. Has there been a time when everything around you felt chaotic or hopeless, yet in the midst of it all, you found a spark of joy? Maybe it was a kind word from a friend, a moment of laughter, or a realization of God's faithfulness. These moments remind us that joy is always accessible when we choose to focus on God rather than our circumstances.

Practical Ways to Choose Joy

Joy is not a passive emotion; it's an active decision to see beyond the pain and trust in God's promises. Choosing joy doesn't mean denying your pain. It means acknowledging it while also embracing the truth that God is greater than your struggles. It's a powerful act of faith that says, "I trust You, Lord, even here, even now, in this seemingly desperate place." This joy becomes our shield, protecting our hearts from the lies of hopelessness and despair.

Practically speaking, cultivating joy can start with small, intentional actions:

1. Begin your day by listing three things you're grateful for. These don't have to be monumental; they can be as simple as a warm cup of coffee, a sunny day, or the sound of birds chirping outside your window. Gratitude is the foundation of joy because it shifts your focus from what's lacking to what's abundant in your life.

2. Nurture joy through worship. Sing praises to God, even when you don't feel like it. Worship has a way of lifting your spirit and aligning your heart with God's truth.

3. Remember Nehemiah's words to the Israelites as they faced opposition while rebuilding Jerusalem's walls: "The joy of the Lord is your strength." (Nehemiah 8:10) This joy wasn't based on their circumstances but on their relationship with God.

Imagine your life as a garden. Pain and struggle may have planted weeds of doubt and despair, but joy is the seed that pushes through the soil, reaching for the light. With care, attention, and trust in God, that seed grows into something beautiful and life-giving. Every time you choose joy, you tend to your garden, allowing it to flourish despite the weeds.

Exiting Hell Moment

Hell thrives on hopelessness, convincing you that joy is out of reach. But joy dismantles despair. Each time you find something to be grateful for, each time you laugh despite your struggles, you're declaring victory over the darkness. Picture joy as a flame that lights your path forward, burning away the lies that tell you joy isn't for you. **Inhale** God's truth and e**xhale** the lie. The joy of the Lord *is* your strength.

Affirmation

The joy of the Lord is my strength, an inexhaustible wellspring of divine power that flows through me even in the darkest valleys and most challenging seasons of my journey. I choose joy today with unwavering determination, knowing that this supernatural gladness transcends my circumstances, defies my enemies, and connects my heart to the eternal delight of my Heavenly Father who rejoices over me with singing and whose presence fills my life with purpose and peace beyond all understanding.

Action Step/Journal Prompt

Write down three things that bring you joy, no matter how small. Make a plan to incorporate one of those things into your day today. Reflect on how it feels to prioritize joy even in difficult times.

Day 8: Don't Contemplate What Might Have Been

Scripture Focus

"Forget the former things; do not dwell on the past. See, I am doing a new thing! Now it springs up; do you not perceive it?" — Isaiah 43:18-19 (NIV)

Reflection

God does not want us to keep looking behind us. How can we move forward if we are spending our time looking behind us? It's time to make a conscious decision to look ahead and focus on what's in front of us—our future, rising to our full potential. God has called us to do mighty things. The only way to accomplish what God has called us to is to keep moving forward. It's the only way if we want to align with God's will for our lives. Don't waste time thinking about what could have been; about what you should've done; about what you would've done. Move forward with speed and boldness.

The Danger of Looking Back

Everyone faces situations of trial, suffering, and grief. God promises that even in these seasons, He is at work. When you are at your lowest ebb, He is there. When you are at your highest high, He is there. It is His loving kindness and compassion that lifts the sense of hopelessness and the weight of despair. Every morning, He gives fresh mercies that sustain and encourage the weary just like He did for the Israelites in the desert. Our manna is the bread of His Word.

Sometimes we have to let go of situations and stop wanting what isn't anymore. Letting go of "old dreams" and previous situations opens the door and makes space for something new. Whenever something seems to come to an end, know that it is actually the start of a new beginning. Even Jesus, while on the cross, stated: "It is finished." Redemption could only come when the work of the old was complete. Take hope. The hearth will not remain cold and full of gritty ash. He will rekindle the flame once again.

Breaking Free from the Past

Remember Lot's wife in Genesis 19? When fleeing from the destruction of Sodom and Gomorrah, she was instructed not to look back. But she couldn't resist. That backward glance—that moment of contemplating what was being left behind caused her to be turned into a pillar of salt. While this story is dramatic, it vividly illustrates the danger of being so fixated on what we're leaving behind that we become frozen, unable to move into what God has prepared ahead.

Paul understood this principle well. In Philippians 3:13-14 (NIV), he writes, "But one thing I do: Forgetting what is behind and straining toward what is ahead, I press on toward the goal to win the prize for which God has called me heavenward in Christ Jesus." Paul had plenty he could have dwelled on—his past sins, his persecution of Christians, the hardships he'd endured. Yet he chose to focus forward, knowing that looking back would only slow his progress.

The Cost of What-Ifs

What exactly happens when we contemplate what might have been? More than just wasting time. It:

1. **Steals our joy in the present.** When we're mentally living in an alternate reality, we miss the gifts God is giving us right now.

2. **Prevents healing.** Wounds can't close when we're constantly reopening them with thoughts of how things could have been different.

3. **Distorts our memory.** Over time, "what might have been" often becomes idealized and unrealistic, making our actual life seem disappointing by comparison.

4. **Dishonors God's sovereignty.** When we obsess over alternate paths, we're essentially saying we know better than God about how our lives should have unfolded.

5. **Paralyzes our progress.** Energy spent contemplating the past is energy not invested in building the future.

Tomorrow is not promised to any of us. Each moment spent looking backward is a moment lost moving forward. Besides, if God intended for us to spend all of our time looking backward, He would have put our eyes on the back of our heads and turned our feet around!

Practical Steps to Focus Forward

How do we train our minds to stop the cycle of "what might have been" thinking? Here are some practical steps:

1. **Capture Your Thoughts.** 2 Corinthians 10:5 tells us to "take captive every thought to make it obedient to Christ." When you catch yourself dwelling on the past, consciously redirect your thinking.

2. **Create a "Thought Boundary."** Decide on a specific, limited time—perhaps 5 minutes—to acknowledge feelings about the past. When that time is up, deliberately shift your focus forward.

3. **Replace "What If" with "What Is."** Instead of asking, "What if I had chosen differently?" ask, "What is God doing in my life right now that I can be grateful for?"

4. **Develop Future-focused Habits.** Start a vision board, set new goals, or create a bucket list that gives you exciting milestones to work toward.

5. **Study God's Faithfulness.** When you're tempted to fixate on the past, open your Bible and read about God's faithfulness to His people through history. Let these stories remind you that He is equally faithful to you now and in the future.

A New Beginning

The beauty of God's promise in Isaiah 43:18-19 is that He isn't just asking us to forget the past—He's promising to do something new. He's springing forth new opportunities, new relationships, new ministry, new joy. If we're looking backward instead of forward, we might miss His right now.

When farmers plow fields, they keep their eyes fixed on a point ahead of them to ensure they create straight furrows. If they kept looking behind to see where they'd been, their rows would become crooked and their work compromised. Even if they look down, right in front of the tractor, their perspective would be skewed and their work less than perfect. The same principle applies to our lives. Fix your eyes on Jesus—the author and perfecter of your faith—who is always before you, never behind.

Exiting Hell Moment

The hell of "what might have been" is like being trapped in a room of mirrors reflecting distorted versions of your past. Today, shatter those mirrors. Feel the liberation of stepping out of that claustrophobic space into the wide-open fields of God's future for you. With each forward step, *inhale* the fresh air of possibility and *exhale* the stale remnants of regret.

Picture yourself standing at a threshold. Behind you is the darkness of "what might have been"—a maze of regrets, hypotheticals, and idealized memories. Before you are the light of what will be—God's plans unfolding day by day. Choose to step forward into the light. Though the path ahead may not be clear, trust that the One leading you sees perfectly. His hand is extended toward you, not behind you.

Affirmation

I choose to focus forward, not backward, releasing the weight of yesterday's failures and disappointments to embrace the limitless possibilities that lie ahead on the path God has prepared for me.

Yesterday is gone. God's mercies are new every morning, cascading over me like a cleansing waterfall that washes away every stain of regret and renews my vision to clearly see the fresh work He is doing in my life today—a divine masterpiece unfolding with perfect timing and purpose that will transform my greatest challenges into my most powerful testimony.

Action Step/Journal Prompt

1. Write down three specific "what might have been" thoughts that frequently occupy your mind

2. For each one, write a prayer surrendering that alternate path to God and asking for His peace.

3. Create a "Forward Focus" list of five things you're looking forward to or working toward in your future.

4. Each time this week that you catch yourself slipping into "what might have been" thinking, immediately redirect your thoughts to one item on your Forward Focus list.

Day 9: Finding Renewal When You're Weary

Scripture Focus

"But they that wait upon the Lord shall renew their strength; they shall mount up with wings as eagles; they shall run and not be weary; and they shall walk, and not faint." — Isaiah 40:31

Reflection

There are days when exhaustion takes over—mentally, emotionally, physically, and spiritually. You try to keep going, but the weight of life feels too heavy. In these moments, you need to remember that your strength does not come from within; it comes from God. It's in your weakness that he's made strong. Until you come to the end of yourself, you're operating on a finite source of strength. At the end of you is the beginning of Him, the infinite source of our strength.

Elijah was a mighty prophet, but he even experienced deep exhaustion. After a great victory against the prophets of Baal, he found himself running for his life, drained and discouraged. He collapsed under a tree and prayed to die. But God met him there, providing food, rest, and reassurance (1 Kings 19:4-8). God didn't criticize Elijah for being weary—He strengthened him for the journey ahead.

The Cycle of Weariness and Renewal

Life often moves in cycles of expenditure and renewal. We pour ourselves out in service, work, relationships, and responsibilities. Eventually, our reserves run low or are completely depleted. This isn't a sign of failure or weakness—it's simply part of the human experience. Even Jesus found it necessary to withdraw regularly to pray and rest, understanding the importance of renewal.

The danger comes when we ignore our need for renewal and push forward on empty. We live in a culture that often glorifies busyness and exhaustion as badges of honor. When I was first building a business, my partners and I would say things like, "I'll sleep when I'm dead" and "we work 8 to faint." Ridiculousness. "I'm so busy" became a status symbol rather than a warning sign. God's design for our lives includes rhythms of work and rest, giving and receiving, pouring out and being filled.

Signs You Need Divine Renewal

How do you know when you're in need of God's renewing strength? Watch for these indicators:

- Small challenges feel overwhelming
- Your emotional responses are disproportionate to situations
- Prayer and spiritual disciplines feel like burdens rather than lifelines
- You find yourself easily irritated or discouraged
- Creative thinking and problem-solving become difficult
- You're making decisions from a place of fear rather than faith

These are not signs of failure but invitations to draw nearer to God who renews our strength.

God's Approach to Our Weariness

Notice how God responded to Elijah's exhaustion. He didn't lecture him about having more faith. He didn't tell him to "push through" or "snap out of it." Instead, God's first response was to meet Elijah's physical needs—rest and nourishment. Only after Elijah was strengthened physically did God speak to him spiritually.

This teaches us something profound about God's approach to our weariness. He cares about our whole being—body, mind, and spirit. Sometimes the most spiritual thing we can do is take a nap, eat a nutritious meal, or take a walk in nature. These aren't distractions from spiritual renewal; they're often the foundation for it.

How to Receive God's Strength

If you feel worn out, here's how to receive God's strength:

1. **Acknowledge Your Need** – Don't push through on your own. Admit when you are struggling and ask God for help. Pride often keeps us from admitting our limitations, but humility opens the door to God's strength.

2. **Rest in Him** – Spiritual and physical rest are essential. Allow yourself to pause and recharge. Create boundaries that protect your time for renewal.

3. **Renew Your Mind** – Replace exhaustion-driven negative thoughts with God's promises of strength. Our thought patterns can either deplete or replenish our energy.

4. **Lean on Community** – Let others support you in prayer and encouragement. We weren't designed to face life's challenges alone.

5. **Take One Step at a Time** – You don't have to have it all figured out. Trust God with each small step forward. Progress in seasons of weariness often comes through small, faithful actions rather than grand gestures.

The Promise of Soaring

Isaiah 40:31 doesn't just promise that we won't collapse; it promises that we will soar. "They will soar on wings like eagles" paints a picture of effortless strength, of being carried by currents higher than we could reach on our own. Eagles don't struggle and flap constantly—they spread their wings and allow the wind to lift them.

This is how God's strength works in our lives. We don't generate it through our own efforts. We position ourselves to receive it by spreading our wings of faith and allowing His Spirit to lift us. Sometimes the most productive thing we can do is to stop striving and start receiving.

Exiting Hell Moment

Weariness can feel like a prison, draining your hope. Today, receive God's strength. Let Him carry what is too heavy for you. ***Exhale*** exhaustion and ***inhale*** His power.

The hell of trying to be strong enough on your own is a prison with walls made of pride and fear. Step out of that prison today. Release the burden of self-sufficiency and embrace the freedom of dependence on God's unlimited strength. As you do, you'll find that the prison doors were never locked—they were only held shut by your reluctance to admit your need.

Affirmation

The Lord renews my strength with divine power that surges through my entire being, replacing my exhaustion with supernatural energy and transforming my weakness into heaven-sent resilience that never diminishes. I will soar on wings like eagles above every obstacle that attempts to ground me, run the race marked out for me without growing weary or losing heart, and walk forward in unwavering faith that propels me through each valley and mountaintop with the absolute certainty that my God orchestrates every step of my journey for His glory and my ultimate good.

Action Step/Journal Prompt

Write about an area in your life where you feel weary. Ask God to strengthen you, then list three practical ways you can position yourself to be renewed physically, emotionally, and spiritually. Make a commitment to implement at least one of these practices as a first step toward embracing God's rhythm of renewal.

Day 10: Cure Loneliness with Solitude

Scripture Focus

"But Jesus often withdrew to lonely places and prayed." — Luke 5:16 (NIV)

Reflection

Life presents many situations that can lead to feelings of loneliness. Perhaps you've moved to a new city where you don't know anyone. Maybe your work keeps you isolated or requires constant travel. You might be facing an empty nest as children leave home. Maybe you're experiencing the loss of a loved one. Some find themselves feeling lonely even in a crowd, disconnected despite being surrounded by others. Whatever your situation, you may now be experiencing feelings of loneliness. It is important, during this time, to recognize the difference between loneliness and solitude. It's crucial for your spiritual and emotional wellbeing.

Loneliness is:

1. Affected with, characterized by, or causing a depressing feeling of being alone; lonesome

2. Destitute of sympathetic or friendly companionship, intercourse, support, etc.: a lonely exile.

3. Lone; solitary; without company; companionless.

While solitude is defined as:

1. The state of being or living alone; seclusion: to enjoy one's solitude.

2. Remoteness from habitations, as of a place; absence of human activity: the solitude of the mountains.

3. A lonely, unfrequented place: solitude in the mountains.

The Difference is Perspective

While loneliness and solitude are the same physical state, it carries the state of being by yourself, isolated from other human beings. Loneliness carries the pain of being alone, while solitude is the joy of being alone. It's all in how you perceive it. Your attitude will determine whether your state is loneliness or solitude.

A lonely person will feel uncared for, unwanted, unloved; they will feel that they lack close contact with others and feel deserted and alone. A person who does not feel lonely will value their solitude as a time when they may work, think, or rest. They will enjoy the privacy and connection to Jesus. They will love the quiet and ability to communicate with God and listen for the still small voice of Holy Spirit that their solitude provides.

From Loneliness to Solitude

Now that we understand the difference between solitude and loneliness, how do we cure our loneliness and fill it with solitude?

1. **Change Your Perspective** - Just because you find yourself in a period of aloneness doesn't mean you have to feel lonely. Don't let other people make you feel ashamed for being alone. Realize that it is better to embrace solitude than to fill your life with meaningless distractions or unhealthy connections.

2. **Balance Community and Solitude** - Immersing yourself in both group and individual activities can help cure loneliness. Reconnect with God; your spirituality is a beneficial way to help cure loneliness.

3. **Serve Others** - Volunteering for a cause will help you accomplish excellent work and think of people (or animals, or issues) beyond yourself. Service breaks the cycle of self-focus that often fuels loneliness.

4. **Befriend Yourself** - Be comfortable spending time with yourself. Use this season to discover more about yourself. What are your interests, passions, and dreams? What brings you joy? What have you always wanted to try but never had the time?

The Sacred Practice of Solitude

Throughout Scripture, we see examples of those who embraced solitude. Jesus Himself "often withdrew to lonely places and prayed" (Luke 5:16). He knew the value of stepping away from crowds and demands of the ministry to commune with His Father. Moses encountered God in the solitude of the burning bush. Elijah heard God's still, small voice not in the earthquake or fire, but in the quiet that followed. David wrote many of his most profound psalms in the solitude of fields and caves.

In 1 Kings 19, after his great victory over the prophets of Baal, Elijah fled into the wilderness alone, exhausted, and afraid. God met him there not with rebuke but with nourishment, rest, and ultimately, His presence in "a gentle whisper" (1 Kings 19:12). It was in this solitude that Elijah received new direction and renewed strength.

Solitude isn't just about being physically alone—it's about creating space for God to speak and move in your life. It's in these quiet moments that many of life's deepest revelations occur.

The desert fathers and mothers of early Christianity deliberately sought solitude, not as punishment but as privilege. This was their chance to strip away distractions and focus wholly on God. They discovered that what begins as apparent emptiness eventually reveals itself as fullness in the presence of God.

The Gift of Solitude

Solitude offers gifts that constant companionship cannot provide:

- **Authentic self-discovery** - In solitude, the masks we wear for others fall away, revealing who we truly are

- **Deeper divine connection** - Without the noise of other voices, God's whisper becomes clearer

- **Emotional processing** - Solitude gives space to feel our feelings without judgment or explanation

- **Mental clarity** - The quiet allows scattered thoughts to settle, bringing wisdom and insight

- **Spiritual renewal** - The soul, like soil, sometimes needs to lie fallow to restore its fertility

- **Creative inspiration** - Many of history's greatest works of art, literature, and spiritual insight were born in solitude

Modern psychology confirms what spiritual traditions have always known: healthy solitude is essential for psychological wellbeing. It is not withdrawal from life but preparation for more meaningful engagement with it.

Practical Steps Forward

If loneliness has become your companion, try these practices to transform it into life-giving solitude:

1. **Create sacred space** - Designate a corner of your home for quiet reflection, prayer, or meditation

2. **Establish routines** - Begin and end your day with intentional moments of solitude and connection with God

3. **Embrace nature** - The natural world offers a unique form of companionship that can ease loneliness

4. **Practice presence** - When alone, resist the urge to fill the silence with noise; simply be where you are

5. **Journal your journey** - Writing helps transform vague feelings into concrete insights

6. **Study solitude** - Read what spiritual teachers have written about the gifts of being alone with God

Exiting Hell Moment

The hell of loneliness is a prison of painful isolation, but the door to freedom is unlocked through a change in perspective. Today, choose to see your alone time not as abandonment but as invitation. Step out of the prison of loneliness and into the garden of solitude, where God awaits to commune with you, heal you, and reveal more of Himself to you.

Remember that the very same circumstances can be experienced as either crushing loneliness or sacred solitude. The difference lies not in the situation but in how you perceive it. As you shift your perspective, what once felt like absence becomes Presence, what seemed like emptiness reveals itself as fullness, and what appeared as abandonment transforms into divine appointment.

Affirmation

Today, I will change my mindset, discarding limiting perspectives that have clouded my vision and embracing transformative truths that illuminate my path with clarity and purpose. I am not alone; I am enjoying my solitude—a sacred space where I discover the richness of my own company, hear God's voice with greater clarity, and cultivate the inner strength that prepares me for meaningful connection with others when the season is right.

Action Step/Journal Prompt

Create a "Solitude Plan" for this week. Schedule at least three 30-minute periods where you will intentionally embrace solitude. For each session, decide on an activity that nurtures your soul—prayer, journaling, reading Scripture, taking a nature walk, or simply sitting quietly. After each session, write down what you discovered about yourself and about God in that time.

Phase 2: Inner Transformation (Days 11-20)

Day 11: God Will Restore All You Lost

Scripture Focus

"And I will restore to you the years that the swarming locust has eaten, the cankerworm, and the caterpillar, and the palmerworm, my great army which I sent among you." — Joel 2:25

Reflection

Loss is one of the most painful experiences we endure. Whether it's the loss of a relationship, opportunity, time, money or even a sense of purpose, loss leaves us feeling empty and hopeless. Thank God that He is a restorer. He specializes in bringing beauty from that which seemed beyond repair.

In the book of Joel, God promised Israel that He would restore the years that had been stolen from them. Having endured devastation, God assured them that restoration was coming. This promise wasn't just about material blessings, it was about renewal, healing, and a fresh start.

Maybe you've lost years to poor decisions, to circumstances beyond your control, or to pain that kept you stuck. Maybe you feel like too much time has passed for things to be restored. Thankfully God does not operate on human timelines. He can take what was broken and make it whole again. He can restore lost time by accelerating blessings, opening new doors, and bringing opportunities you never imagined. He can even reverse the aging process! He renews your youth like the eagles!! (Psalm 103:5). Once again, with all we encountered in our youth, we can be left feeling depleted, physically and emotionally. God, in His infinite wisdom, has already provided for our restoration.

Understanding God's Heart for Restoration

Restoration is not just something God does—it's a reflection of who He is. Throughout Scripture, we see His Heart is to restore what was lost, broken, or stolen. He is the God who leaves the ninety-nine to find the one lost sheep (Luke 15:3-7). He is the Father who runs to embrace the prodigal son who squandered his inheritance (Luke 15:11-32). He is the Redeemer who restores His people despite their unfaithfulness (Hosea 3:1-5).

The very story of salvation is one of restoration—God sent Jesus, His own son, to restore the relationship with humanity that was broken in the Garden of Eden. Who could honestly say they would be able to express love like this? Jesus came to "seek and save the lost" (Luke 19:10), the same people who were yelling, "Crucify Him," demonstrating God's unwavering commitment to restoration. His death and resurrection made possible the ultimate restoration: reconciliation between God and humanity. I am reminded of the scars in His hands. Scars that tell the story of how He overcame on our behalf.

God's restoration is always greater than the original loss. He doesn't just repair—He transforms. He doesn't just replace—He upgrades. He takes the broken pieces of our lives and creates a mosaic more beautiful than before, where even the fracture lines tell a story of His redemptive power.

Biblical Examples of Restoration

Think of Job. He lost everything, his wealth, his health, and even his children. Yet, because he remained faithful, refusing to murmur and complain, never agreed with the naysayers who told him to curse God and die, God gave him a double portion of all he had lost (Job 42:10). What the enemy meant for harm; God turned for his good (Genesis 50:20). Job's story reminds us that even in our darkest moments, restoration is possible.

Consider Joseph. His own brothers sold him into slavery because they were jealous of his relationship with their father. He endured years of servitude and imprisonment, separated from his family and homeland.

There were many dark and lonely nights where, I would imagine, Joseph wondered why me, why now? Has God completely forgotten about me. You know, the same thoughts we have. Yet God was with him through it all, eventually elevating him to a position of authority that allowed him to save many lives including the lives of those who enslaved him for money, his own family. What looked like a devastating loss became the vehicle for tremendous blessing and redemption.

Ruth and Naomi experienced profound loss. Both were widowed and Naomi lost her sons. They returned to Bethlehem empty and grieving. Yet God orchestrated a beautiful restoration, after tremendous sorrow, through Ruth's marriage to Boaz, providing not only for their immediate needs but also placing Ruth in the lineage of King David and ultimately, Jesus Christ. Their story shows how God can restore hope when all seems lost.

King David, after his moral failure with Bathsheba, experienced the painful consequences of his sin. Yet God restored him, not by removing those consequences, but by extending forgiveness, renewing his spirit, and continuing to use him as a man after God's own heart. His story reminds us that God's restoration often comes through, not around, our failures and pain.

The Nature of Divine Restoration

The nature of divine restoration is such that it doesn't always look like we expect. Sometimes, God restores relationships. Other times, He gives us something new to replace what was lost. His restoration is always better than what we could have imagined for ourselves.

God's restoration may not come immediately. Actually, it may not come for what seems to be a long, long time. There may be a season of waiting, a desert experience, or a time of preparation before restoration manifests. During this time, God is often working beneath the surface—in your heart, in circumstances, or in the hearts of others—preparing the way for restoration. Just as a farmer must prepare the soil before planting, God prepares us to receive and steward what He wants to restore.

God's restoration comes in unexpected ways. You may be praying for the restoration of a specific relationship, but God may instead bring new, healthier relationships into your life. You might be seeking restoration of a lost opportunity, but God may open an entirely new door you never imagined. His ways are higher than our ways, and His thoughts higher than our thoughts (Isaiah 55:9).

The Process of Restoration

Restoration is rarely instantaneous—it's typically a process that unfolds over time. Just as the Israelites had to participate in their restoration by returning to the land, replanting vineyards, and rebuilding cities, we often play an active role in our own restoration.

Part of this process involves healing. Before true restoration can occur, the wounds of loss must be addressed. God doesn't just cover our pain, nor does He want us to. We want to act as if certain things never happened while God wants us completely healed from the inside out. This may involve facing painful truths, forgiving those who hurt you, or releasing dreams that just weren't meant to be. Like a skilled physician, God doesn't just treat symptoms; He addresses root causes in order to bring total and complete healing and restoration.

Another aspect of restoration is reframing. God helps us see our losses in a new light—not minimizing the pain, but revealing how He can work through it. Romans 8:28 reminds us that "All things work together for good to them that love God, to them who ae called according to his purpose." This doesn't mean the loss in and of itself was good, it means that God will redeem it and incorporate it into His plan for your life.

Restoration often involves rebuilding. Sometimes literally, as when the Israelites rebuilt Jerusalem's walls under Nehemiah's leadership. Other times figuratively, as we establish new patterns, create new connections, or develop new habits and perspectives. God often partners with us in this rebuilding process, providing wisdom, strength, and resources while inviting our participation.

Embracing God's Restoration

Here's how to embrace God's restoration in your life:

1. **Believe That Restoration is Possible** – Doubt can keep you from receiving what God wants to give you. Trust that He is both able and willing to positively affect whatever situation you are facing. Faith opens the door for God's restoration power to flow into your situation.

2. **Let Go of the Past** – You cannot step into restoration while holding onto resentment, regret, or despair. Release it to God. Surrender what was lost and make room for what God wants to bless you.

3. **Be Open to a New Thing** – Sometimes, God restores by giving you something better than what you lost. Isaiah 43:19 says, "See, I am doing a new thing! Now it springs up; do you not perceive it?" Be willing to embrace God's "new thing," even if it differs from what you expected.

4. **Declare Restoration Over Your Life** – Speak Joel 2:25 over your situation and expect God to move. There is power in aligning your words with God's promises and speaking them by faith into manifestation.

5. **Position Yourself for Blessings** – Stay obedient, faithful, and ready to receive what God has for you. Like the servants at the wedding in Cana who filled the water jars (John 2:1-11), your obedience positions you to witness God's miraculous restoration.

6. **Practice Patience** – Restoration often unfolds gradually. The farmers mentioned in James 5:7 had to wait patiently for the land to yield its valuable crop. Similarly, you may have to wait for God's perfect timing to see the restoration you seek.

7. **Despise not Small Beginnings** – Like Elijah who saw a cloud the size of a man's hand (1 Kings 18:41-45), learn to recognize the small beginnings of God's restoration. Celebrate these signs and let them strengthen your faith for the greater restoration to come.

Testimonies of Restoration

Throughout history, believers have experienced God's incredible restoration power. Consider the testimony of Corrie ten Boom, who lost her family and freedom in Nazi concentration camps yet later found the strength to forgive her captors and established a worldwide ministry of healing and restoration. Or think of Joni Eareckson Tada, whose paralysis could have ended her dreams but instead became the platform for a ministry that has touched millions.

Perhaps you know someone who has experienced divine restoration—a marriage rebuilt after betrayal, a career reestablished after failure, health restored after illness, or faith rekindled after doubt. These testimonies remind us that God is still in the restoration business today.

Your own life will become a testimony of God's restoration power. The very areas where you've experienced the greatest loss will become the strongest evidence of His faithfulness. As Joel 2:26 promises, "You will have plenty to eat, until you are full, and you will praise the name of the LORD your God, who has worked wonders for you."

Exiting Hell Moment

Loss can feel like a prison, trapping you in grief and regret. But God is the ultimate restorer. Today, trust that He is working behind the scenes to bring restoration into your life. *Inhale* His promise of renewal and *exhale* sorrow.

You are holding the broken pieces of your past, feeling like they can never be put back together. Then, God takes those pieces, reshapes them, and hands you something even more beautiful than before. What was lost is now restored—not just repaired but transformed into something that reflects His glory and advances His kingdom.

The hell of loss tries to convince you that what's gone is gone forever—that your story ends in deficit and disappointment. But God specializes in resurrection. Just as Jesus emerged victorious from the grave, what you thought was dead and buried can rise again through His power. Step out of the grave of grief and into the garden of restoration, where new life is already beginning to bloom.

Affirmation

God has restored what I lost with divine precision and supernatural abundance, weaving together broken threads into a tapestry more beautiful than what was taken from me. He has made all things new in my life—not merely repairing what was damaged but creating something more glorious that reflects His redemptive power and unfailing love. What the enemy meant for harm, God has turned for my good and His glory, transforming my deepest wounds into channels of healing for others and my darkest valleys into platforms where His light shines with unmistakable brilliance that testifies to His sovereignty over every circumstance.

Action Step/Journal Prompt

Write about an area of your life where you have experienced loss. Then, write a declaration of faith that God will restore what has been taken. Keep it where you can see it as a daily reminder.

List three small steps you can take this week to participate in God's restoration process—whether through seeking healing, planting seeds for the future, or preparing to receive what God wants to restore. Let these steps serve as a reminder that God is with you always ... even until the end of time.

Day 12: Trusting God's Timing

Scripture Focus

"He hath made everything beautiful in his time." — Ecclesiastes 3:11

Reflection

Exercising patience is one of life's greatest challenges. In a world that values instant gratification, trusting God's timing requires faith and patience. We know that His timing is perfect, even when it doesn't align with ours. Doesn't make waiting any easier though.

The Purpose in Waiting

Your time in waiting is not wasted time. It's a season of preparation and trust. During the wait, work is going on behind the scenes to align circumstances and prepare your heart in ways you may not yet see. Waiting refines you, teaches patience, and helps to build your faith. It forces you to release control and lean fully on God's promises, knowing that He is orchestrating every detail with divine precision.

As beautiful and delightful to watch as butterflies are, it wasn't always that way. At some point, that beautiful butterfly was an ugly caterpillar in a cocoon. From the outside, it looks like nothing is happening. But inside, a miraculous transformation is underway. If you were to open the cocoon too soon, you would interrupt the process and prevent the butterfly from fully developing. The butterfly needs the process of escaping the cocoon to even strengthen its wings enough to fly. There is a story of three little boys who thought they were helping a butterfly out if its cocoon by peeling away the outer layers that kept it bound. That butterfly never flew. Without going through its entire process, the butterfly's wings were not strengthened enough to support their body weight and as a result, they never lived their complete destiny. The same is true with God's timing— when you try to rush His process, you might miss the full beauty of what He is creating in you.

Cultural Impatience vs. Divine Timing

Waiting often feels uncomfortable because we live in a culture that prioritizes immediacy. When we don't see instant results, we assume God is neither involved nor concerned. Consider Abraham and Sarah, who waited decades for God's promise of a child. In their impatience, they took matters into their own hands, leading to unnecessary complications. Even in their error, God's promise was not voided. In His perfect timing, Isaac was born, proving that His promises never fail.

Trust that His timing is not just good—it's perfect. Every delay, every closed door, each moment of stillness is purposeful. God is setting things in motion, refining your character, and preparing the way for blessings ahead. Waiting is not about stagnation; it's about transformation. In the waiting, God is shaping you into who He created you to be, ensuring that when the time is right, you will be fully ready to step into His plans.

Biblical Examples of Divine Timing

Scripture is filled with stories of God's perfect timing. Consider Joseph, who spent years as a slave and prisoner before his divine appointment as Egypt's second-in-command. Those years weren't wasted; they were preparation. Through hardship, Joseph developed the character, wisdom, and humility necessary to handle the position God had planned for him to impact nations.

Moses spent forty years in the wilderness before God called him to lead Israel out of Egypt. During that time, the proud prince of Egypt became the humble shepherd who could hear God's voice. The wilderness wasn't a detour; it was God's training ground.

David was anointed king as a young man but didn't take the throne until many years later. The period between his anointing and coronation was filled with challenges, including being hunted by his very own trusted mentor, King Saul. Yet during this time, David learned to depend on God, developed leadership skills and wrote many of the Psalms that continue to comfort believers today.

Even Jesus had His time of waiting. Before beginning His public ministry at age thirty, He spent decades in relative obscurity, working as a carpenter. The Son of God Himself submitted to the Father's timing.

The Waiting Room: A Place of Growth

Think of waiting as sitting in God's waiting room. The waiting room isn't a punishment; it's a place of preparation. Our job is to simply "wait well." In this space, God may be:

1. **Developing Your Character** — Waiting builds perseverance, which James 1:4 tells us leads to maturity and completeness.

2. **Aligning Circumstances** — Just as a master chess player plans several moves ahead, God is orchestrating events and people in ways we cannot see.

3. **Protecting You** — Sometimes God's "not yet" is protection from something you're not ready to handle or a situation that isn't ready for you.

4. **Testing Your Faith** — Will you trust Him even when you can't see the outcome?

5. **Teaching Dependence** — In our waiting, we learn that our strength and wisdom are insufficient; we need God's guidance and power.

Practical Ways to Wait Well

How do we wait without becoming bitter or discouraged? Here are some practical steps:

1. **Stay in God's Word** — Feed your faith with Scripture that reminds you of God's faithfulness and perfect timing.

2. **Maintain a Posture of Worship** — Like David, who praised God while waiting to become king, choose to focus on who God is rather than what He hasn't yet done.

3. **Serve Others** — Instead of fixating on your own waiting, look for ways to be a blessing to those around you.

4. **Embrace the Present** — Don't miss the gifts of today by constantly looking toward tomorrow.

5. **Keep a Gratitude Journal** — Write down daily blessings to maintain perspective during the wait.

6. **Seek Godly Counsel** — Sometimes we need others to help us see God's work when our vision is clouded by impatience.

When the Wait Seems Endless

Perhaps you've been waiting for years—for healing, for a relationship to be restored, for a dream to be fulfilled. The longer the wait, the harder it can be to maintain hope. In those moments, remember that God is not bound by our timelines. His concept of timing is different from ours, as 2 Peter 3:8 reminds us: "With the Lord a day is like a thousand years, and a thousand years are like a day."

Consider the nation of Israel, who waited 400 years in Egyptian slavery before Moses came to deliver them. They waited 40 more years in the wilderness before entering the Promised Land. Later, they waited centuries for the promised Messiah. Yet in each case, God's timing was perfect. When Jesus finally came, it was, as Galatians 4:4 tells us, "In the fullness of time"—exactly when all conditions were right.

Sometimes our waiting is prolonged because we're looking for a certain outcome and God has actually worked it out in another way. We pray for a door to open but He may be using the closed door to direct us toward a better path. We ask for immediate relief from a situation, when that very situation may be what God is using to produce something of far greater value in our lives.

When You're Tempted to Rush Ahead

The temptation to take matters into our own hands, like Abraham and Sarah did, can be overwhelming. We think, "Maybe God needs my help," or "Perhaps God has forgotten His promise." But rushing ahead of God's timing often creates greater complications rather than solutions.

King Saul couldn't wait for Samuel to arrive to offer the sacrifice before battle, so he took on the priest's role himself—a decision that cost him the kingdom. The Israelites couldn't wait for Moses to come down from Mount Sinai, so they created a golden calf—leading to devastating consequences.

When you feel the urge to rush ahead, pause and pray for renewed trust. Remember that God's delays are not denials. His apparent inaction is never the result of indifference or forgetfulness. He sees you. He hears you. And He is working, even when you can't perceive it.

Exiting Hell Moment

Impatience can feel like its own hell, stealing your peace. Today, surrender your timeline to God and trust that He is working all things for your good. ***Exhale*** frustration and ***inhale*** trust. Let go of the need to control the when and how of God's work in your life. As you release your grip on your own expectations, you'll find yourself stepping out of the prison of anxiety and into the freedom of faith.

Picture yourself standing at a scenic overlook, watching the sun rise. You can't rush the sun—it moves at its own pace, gradually illuminating the landscape. As you wait patiently, the beauty unfolds before you, revealing details and colors you couldn't see in the darkness. God's timing works the same way, gradually revealing His perfect plan, with each moment of waiting bringing new understanding and beauty.

Affirmation

God's timing is perfect, orchestrating every detail of my life with divine precision that transcends my limited understanding. I trust Him completely to make everything beautiful in its time, resting in the certainty that He weaves delays, detours, and even disappointments into a masterpiece of purpose that will ultimately reveal His glory and my good.

Action Step/Journal Prompt

Write about something you are waiting for. Reflect on how God might be using this season to prepare you. Pray for patience and trust in His timing. Then, make a list of five specific ways you can "wait well" this week, actively trusting God while you await His perfect timing.

Day 13: Embracing New Beginnings

Scripture Focus

"Therefore, if any man be in Christ, he is a new creature: old things are passed away; behold, all things are become new." — 2 Corinthians 5:17

Reflection

New beginnings are a gift from God, an opportunity to start fresh and leave the past behind. Embracing them requires courage and faith, but the reward is a life aligned with His purpose. Often, stepping into something new means letting go of the old—past mistakes, regrets, or even successes that no longer serve the path God has laid before you.

Peter was one of Jesus' closest disciples. He had walked with Jesus, witnessed miracles, and boldly proclaimed his faith. Yet, in Jesus' darkest hour, Peter denied Him—not once, but three times. Imagine the weight of that failure. Peter could have allowed his shame to define him, to retreat into his past, believing he had ruined any chance of fulfilling his purpose. But Jesus, in His infinite grace, restored him. In John 21, we see Jesus giving Peter a fresh start, asking him three times if he loves Him, mirroring Peter's three denials. Jesus didn't just forgive Peter—He reaffirmed his purpose, telling him to "feed my sheep." Peter's story reminds us that failure is not final when God is involved.

God's Promise of Renewal

God is always in the business of renewal. No matter what has happened before, He offers you the chance to start again. Isaiah 43:18-19 says, "Forget the former things; do not dwell on the past. See, I am doing a new thing! Now it springs up; do you not perceive it?" God is continually at work in your life, creating new opportunities for growth, healing, and purpose.

Sometimes, new beginnings feel overwhelming. Change can be uncomfortable, and stepping into the unknown requires faith. It's like standing on the edge of a river, knowing you need to cross but feeling unsure about the strength of the bridge. This is where trust in God comes in. Proverbs 3:5-6 reminds us, "Trust in the Lord with all thine heart; and lean not on your own understanding. In all thy ways submit to Him, and He will make your paths straight." When you trust God, He will direct your steps, even when you can't see the whole path ahead.

Finding Courage to Move Forward

Consider a woman who had spent years in a toxic relationship, believing she wasn't worthy of anything better. When she finally walked away, she felt lost. The familiarity of her past was gone, and the uncertainty of her future seemed daunting. However, as she leaned into God, she found the strength to rebuild. She developed new habits, deepened her faith, and surrounded herself with people who encouraged her. Over time, she realized that her new beginning was not something to fear but a divine invitation to walk in freedom.

What new beginning is God offering you? It might be a fresh start in a relationship, career, mindset, or even your spiritual walk. Maybe you've been stuck in fear, regret, or complacency. Now is the time to embrace the newness God is calling you into.

Practical Steps for New Beginnings

Here are a few ways to embrace a new beginning with faith:

1. **Release the Past** – You can't fully embrace what's ahead if you're holding onto what's behind. Let go of past hurts, failures, or disappointments.

2. **Seek God's Guidance** – Spend time in prayer, asking God for wisdom and clarity about the new path He is leading you on.

3. **Take Small Steps Forward** – New beginnings don't always require giant leaps. Sometimes, it's about making small, intentional steps in the right direction.

4. **Surround Yourself with Encouragement** – Find people who will support you, pray for you, and remind you of God's promises.

5. **Trust God's Process** – Even when things don't unfold the way you expect, trust that God is working everything together for your good. (Romans 8:28)

Exiting Hell Moment

You are standing in a vast field, the morning sun breaking through the darkness. The air is crisp, the possibilities endless. Each step you take forward erases the footprints of your past, leaving you free to walk boldly into your future. This is the power of God's renewal—offering you a fresh start, a new story, and a life aligned with His divine purpose.

Staying stuck in the past is its own hell. Today, choose to step into the new beginning God has for you. ***Inhale*** hope and ***exhale*** regret.

Affirmation

I am a new creation in Christ, completely transformed by His redeeming power that has erased my past and freed me from its grip. The old has gone and the new has come, infusing every part of my being with divine purpose and heavenly identity that cannot be diminished by circumstances or defined by my former failures.

Action Step/Journal Prompt

Write about a new beginning you are stepping into. Reflect on what excites you and what fears you need to surrender to God. Pray for courage and guidance as you embrace this new chapter.

Day 14: Control Your Thinking

What you think about, you ultimately bring about.

Scripture Focus

"When my anxious thoughts multiply within me, your consolations delight my soul." — Psalm 94:19

Reflection

Somewhere I read that a woman's mind is like Internet Explorer opened with 132 tabs, constantly working, constantly thinking, constantly calculating. This is how we are wired, but when those 132 tabs consist of 130 tabs of junk, we are dragging ourselves backward instead of moving forward. We must guard our minds, guard our ears, and guard our hearts.

"Put to death therefore what is earthly in you: sexual immorality, impurity, passion, evil desire, and covetousness, which is idolatry. On account of these the wrath of God is coming. In these you too once walked, when you were living in them. But now you must put them all away: anger, wrath, malice, slander, and obscene talk from your mouth. Do not lie to one another, seeing that you have put off the old self with its practices." Colossians 3:5-10. (ESV)

The Battle for Your Mind

Our thoughts are powerful. They shape our emotions, influence our decisions, and ultimately determine the direction of our lives. Scripture repeatedly emphasizes the importance of guarding our minds and controlling our thoughts. Proverbs 4:23 warns us to guard our hearts (which includes our thoughts), "for everything you do flows from it."

In the journey of healing and moving forward, one of the greatest challenges is controlling the direction of our thoughts. It's easy to fall into patterns of rumination—replaying past hurts, imagining "what if" scenarious or dwelling on negative emotions. These thought patterns not only keep us stuck in pain but can actually deepen our wounds.

Practical Steps for Thought Control

That means you may need to take a step (or leap) away from your ex's mutual friends and family. Get away from those people who, with just a line like "I saw your ex today," can send your mind spinning into turmoil: "What did he look like? Who was he with? Did he look happy?" In order to control your thoughts, you have to control your thoughts and guard your mind.

It takes conscious energy to change your thinking. We have the power to control our thoughts through Holy Spirit; we have the divine power to destroy those strongholds that keep our minds imprisoned. We must keep our minds on Jesus and His presence in our lives.

The Power of Holy Spirit

Second Corinthians 10:5 tells us to "take captive every thought to make it obedient to Christ." This isn't something we accomplish through willpower alone. It requires the supernatural assistance of Holy Spirit working within us. When intrusive thoughts come—whether they're anxious fears about the future or painful memories from the past—we can surrender them to God.

Holy Spirit empowers us to replace destructive thought patterns with life-giving truth. Romans 12:2 encourages us to "be transformed by the renewing of your mind." This transformation happens as we intentionally fill our minds with God's Word, allowing His truth to reshape our thinking.

The Philippians 4:8 "Filter"

If you find yourself having a challenging time controlling your thoughts, ask yourself these questions:

- Am I thinking about things that are true?

- Am I thinking about things that are good?

- Am I thinking thoughts that are pure and of good report?

These questions come directly from Philippians 4:8, which instructs us to think about "whatever is true, whatever is noble, whatever is right, whatever is pure, whatever is lovely, whatever is admirable—if anything is excellent or praiseworthy—think about such things. Whatever you have learned or received or heard from me or seen in me – put it into practice. And the God of peace will be with you." And isn't it peace that we are really after?

This verse gives us a powerful filter through which to process our thoughts. When a thought enters your mind, run it through this filter. Does it align with these qualities? If not, it's a thought that needs to be taken captive and replaced with truth.

The Daily Practice of Thought Control

Controlling your thoughts is a constant battle, a struggle. If you allow Holy Spirit to help, this battle can be won. If you can control your thoughts, you can control your life. One of my mentors said that even if you can't stop the birds from flying over your head, you can definitely stop them from building a nest there. The thoughts will come. It's up to you to dispel them.

Here are some practical ways to strengthen your thought life:

1. **Start your day with Worship and Prayer** - Before your mind gets filled with the day's concerns, fill it with God's truth.

2. **Memorize Key Verses** - When negative thoughts come, having Scripture readily available in your mind gives you ammunition to fight back

3. **Practice Thought-stopping** - When you catch yourself thinking harmful thoughts, say "Stop" (even aloud if necessary), and deliberately redirect your mind.

4. **Create Healthy Thought Routines** - Set aside time each day for gratitude, reflecting on God's goodness, or meditating on a specific truth from Scripture.

5. **Be Mindful of Your Environment** - What you watch, read, and listen to influences your thought life. Choose media that builds up rather than tears down.

God's Consolations for Anxious Thoughts

Psalm 94:19 reminds us that when anxious thoughts multiply within us, God's consolations delight our souls. God doesn't just command us to control our thoughts without providing the means to do so. He offers His consolations—His comfort, His presence, His promises—as the antidote to racing, anxious thoughts.

What are these consolations? They include His promises in Scripture, the presence of His Spirit, the support of His people, and the assurance of His unchanging love. When anxious thoughts begin to multiply, turn to these consolations. Let them fill your mind and delight your soul.

Exiting Hell Moment

The prison of uncontrolled thoughts can feel like a personal hell—a place where your mind torments you with fears, regrets, and painful memories. Today, claim the freedom Christ offers. Begin the practice of taking your thoughts captive. Each time you redirect a negative thought pattern toward God's truth; you're stepping further away from that mental prison and into the freedom of a mind renewed by Christ. *Inhale* possibility. *Exhale* regret.

Affirmation

I will not dwell on the past—for God is doing a new thing in me. I declare that fresh vision, fresh opportunities, and divine surprises are already unfolding in my life. What once felt dry and barren is now springing forth with purpose and possibility. I may not have seen it before, but now I choose to perceive it. My eyes are open, my heart is ready, and my spirit is aligned. I embrace the new, the now, and the next with faith and expectation—because God has already begun!

Action Step/Journal Prompt

Create a "thought inventory" by writing down recurring thoughts that pull you backward instead of forward. Next to each one, write a truth from Scripture that counters it. Commit to reviewing and meditating on these truths daily for the next week, and journal about any changes you notice in your thought patterns.

Day 15: The Power of Your Words

You will have what you say

Scripture Focus

"The tongue has the power of life and death, and those who love it will eat its fruit." — Proverbs 18:21(NIV)

"Words kill, words give life; they're either poison or fruit – you choose." Proverbs 18:21 (MSG)

Reflection

Words shape our world. They can uplift or tear down, heal or wound, build faith or instill fear. Often, we underestimate the power of what we speak over ourselves and others. Scripture tells us that our words hold the power of life and death, meaning they have real, lasting effects on our spiritual, emotional, and mental well-being.

Think about how God created the world—He spoke it into existence. His words had the power to bring forth life, and because we are created in His image, our words carry weight as well. What we declare over our lives influences the direction of our journey.

Negative self-talk, gossip, and doubt are like seeds planted in our hearts and minds. If we constantly speak of failure, fear, or discouragement, we begin to believe those things. On the other hand, when we align our speech with God's truth, we plant seeds of faith, hope, and transformation.

The Destructive and Creative Power of Words

James 3:5-6 compares the tongue to a small spark that can set an entire forest on fire. It may seem like just a few words spoken in anger, self-doubt, or frustration, but those words can have far-reaching consequences. A single sentence can damage a relationship, break trust, or discourage someone from pursuing their God-given purpose.

Our words are like bubbles. Once they're blown, you cannot get them back. They pop! Your words stay with your target forever. On the other hand, words also have the power to bring healing and restoration. Proverbs 16:24 reads, "Gracious words are a honeycomb, sweet to the soul and healing to the bones." Have you ever received an encouraging word at just the right moment? Words have the power to lift spirits, strengthen hearts, and renew hope.

The enemy wants us to misuse our words—to curse ourselves with negativity, to doubt God's promises, and to speak out of anger instead of wisdom. When we intentionally use our words to glorify God, to speak life over our circumstances, and to declare His promises, we shift the atmosphere around us.

Speak Life in Your Situation

Speak life into your situations starting today:

1. **Speak God's Word** – Fill your mouth with Scripture. Instead of saying, "I'm not good enough," declare, "I am fearfully and wonderfully made" (Psalm 139:14).

2. **Reject Negative Talk** – Be mindful of the words you speak over yourself and others. Catch yourself when negativity creeps in.

3. **Encourage and Uplift** – Make it a habit to build up those around you. Your words can be the encouragement someone else needs to keep going. Besides, as an added benefit, you will reap what you sow.

4. **Pray with Power** – When you pray, declare God's promises boldly. Speak as someone who believes in His power.

5. **Declare Victory** – Even in difficult seasons, remind yourself, "God is working this for my good" (Romans 8:28).

Exiting Hell Moment

See yourself holding seeds in your hand. Every word you speak is a seed planted in the soil of your life and the lives of those closest to you. What kind of harvest will your words create? Words of faith, hope, and love will bring forth a garden of blessings. Words of fear, doubt, and negativity will produce weeds that choke out your joy.

If your words have been aligning with fear, failure, or negativity, today is the day to change that. Speak life over your situation. **Inhale** the promises of God and *exhale* defeat.

Affirmation

I am a new creation in Christ, completely transformed by His redeeming power that has erased my past and freed me from its grip. The old has gone and the new has come, infusing every part of my being with divine purpose and heavenly identity that cannot be diminished by circumstances or defined by my former failures.

Action Step/Journal Prompt

Write down three negative things you often say about yourself. Rewrite them into positive, faith-filled declarations based on God's Word. Find the Scripture references and commit them to memory.

Day 16: God's Grace is Enough

In your weakness, He is strong

Scripture Focus

"Therefore, I take pleasure in infirmities, in reproaches, in necessities, in persecutions, in distresses for Christ's sake: for when I am weak, then am I strong." — 2 Corinthians 12:9

Reflection

We live in a world that celebrates strength, independence, and self-sufficiency; a world where everyone boasts of their self-confidence and self-worth. The Kingdom of God operates differently. It is in that Kingdom that we should find our value, our 'God-fidence' if you will. The realization that we cannot be good enough, that we cannot work hard enough to gain the blessings of God – that it is only by grace we are saved through faith – lest any man should boast, helps us to maintain our humility and our reliance on God for everything. His grace is sufficient. In our weakness, His power is made perfect. This means that we don't have to have it all together. We don't have to be the strongest, the smartest, or the most capable. We simply need to rely wholly on Him.

Paul, one of the greatest apostles, struggled with a persistent issue he referred to as a "thorn in the flesh." Despite pleading with God to remove it, God's response was not to take it away but to remind Paul that His grace was sufficient; more than enough. He encouraged Paul that no matter what He faced, God's grace would see him through. This teaches us that grace is not about eliminating the struggle; it is about His sustaining us through all of the struggles.

Understanding God's Grace

Grace is often defined as the unmerited favor of God; more literally, receiving what we don't deserve. Grace is much more than a theological concept. It is the active expression of God's love toward us, empowering us to live beyond our natural capabilities. It is the divine strength that flows into our lives when we acknowledge our need for it.

Grace doesn't just save us; it sustains us. Ephesians 2:8-9 reminds us that it is by grace we are saved, through faith— not by works --- lest any man should boast. We cannot work hard enough for what we receive. This same grace that brought us into relationship with God continues to work, in every area of our lives, transforming us from the inside out. Grace is both God's gift for salvation and His provision for everyday living.

In a performance-oriented culture, grace stands in stark contrast to the message that our value is based on what we achieve. Grace says your worth is already established—not by what you do, but by who you are. You are God's beloved child, and His love for you is not contingent on your performance. You can't be good enough, nor can you work hard enough to deserve the favor of almighty God. It is only through the blood of Jesus Christ that we are justified.

The Beauty of Divine Grace

God's grace covers every failure, every mistake, and every moment of weakness. Think about Peter—he denied Jesus three times, yet Jesus restored him and called him to lead. Grace is not about deserving; it's about God's love being bigger than our shortcomings.

Maybe you feel like you are not enough. Maybe you see your flaws and failures and wonder if God can still use you. The answer is yes—He can and will. God does not require perfection; He requires obedience and surrender.

Consider King David, who committed adultery and murder, yet was still called "a man after God's own heart." How was this possible? Because

David understood grace. When confronted with his sin, he didn't run or hide—he repented and received God's forgiveness. Psalm 51 reveals David's heart: "Create in me a pure heart, O God, and renew a steadfast spirit within me." This is the posture that allows grace to transform us.

When Grace Feels Insufficient

There may be times when you struggle to believe that God's grace is truly enough:

- When you've made the same mistake repeatedly and wonder if you've exhausted God's patience
- When your circumstances don't change despite earnest prayer
- When you feel overwhelmed by life's demands and your own inadequacies
- When others seem to have it all together while you struggle

In these moments, remember that God's grace isn't measured by your feelings or circumstances. Paul's thorn remained, but God's grace sustained him through it. The unchanging nature of your situation doesn't indicate an absence of grace rather an invitation to experience grace in a deeper way.

Practical Ways to Rest in Grace

Here's how to rest in God's grace:

1. **Acknowledge Your Weakness** – Instead of hiding your struggles, bring them to God. James 4:6 tells us that "God opposes the proud but shows favor to the humble." Acknowledging weakness isn't weakness, it's the pathway to strength.

2. **Stop Striving** – God's love is not based on performance. You are loved as you are. Release the exhausting pursuit of earning what has already been freely given to you.

3. **Receive His Strength** – Lean into God's power when you feel weak. This means actively depending on Him rather than relying on your own resources. Ask for His strength in specific situations.

4. **Embrace the Process** – Growth takes time. Allow God's grace to work in you daily. Sanctification is a journey, not an instant transformation. Be patient with yourself as God's grace gradually changes you.

5. **Extend Grace to Others** – As you receive grace, learn to give it freely. Jesus taught that we forgive as we have been forgiven. Your experience of grace deepens as you extend it to others.

6. **Refuse Condemnation** – Reject the lies that say you are not enough. Romans 8:1 declares, "There is therefore now no condemnation to them which are in Christ Jesus..." Learn to distinguish between conviction (which leads to repentance) and condemnation (which leads to shame).

7. **Live in Gratitude** – Let grace remind you of God's goodness daily. Gratitude is the natural response to grace. As you recognize God's unmerited favor in your life, thanksgiving will flow from your heart.

Grace in Community

Grace isn't meant to be experienced in isolation. God often channels His grace through the community of believers. When you struggle to believe grace is enough, sometimes you need others to remind you of this truth. Their encouragement, support, and even correction can be vehicles of grace in your life.

Hebrews 10:24-25 encourages us not to give up meeting together, but to spur one another on toward love and good deeds. In community, we experience grace in tangible ways—through forgiveness, acceptance, and loving accountability. We see grace lived out in the lives of others, giving us hope for our own journey.

Exiting Hell Moment

See yourself holding the broken pieces of your life, feeling like they can never be put back together. Then, God takes those pieces, reshapes them, and hands you something even more beautiful than before. What was broken is now restored. This is the picture of grace—not the absence of brokenness, but the presence of divine strength in the midst of it.

The prison of perfectionism keeps you constantly striving, never resting, always feeling inadequate. God's grace unlocks the door of that prison. Step out of the exhausting cycle of trying to earn what God freely gives. In that moment of surrender, you'll find freedom you never thought possible to be imperfect yet fully loved. ***Exhale*** the lie that you're not enough and ***inhale*** the truth that Christ in you is more than sufficient.

Affirmation

God's grace is sufficient for me. In my weakness, He is strong. I no longer need to strive for approval that has already been given through Christ.

Action Step/Journal Prompt

Write down an area where you have been striving in your own strength. Then, pray and ask God to help you rest in His grace instead of relying on your efforts alone. Throughout the week, note moments when you feel tempted to revert to self-sufficiency, and practice consciously surrendering those moments to God's grace.

Day 17: Walking in Confidence

Scripture Focus

"So do not throw away your confidence; it will be richly rewarded." — Hebrews 10:35 (NIV)

Reflection

Confidence is one of the most powerful tools you can carry on your journey of exiting hell. However, confidence isn't just about believing in yourself; it's about believing in the One who created you. The enemy tries to attack your confidence by planting seeds of doubt, fear, and insecurity, causing you to shrink back from the fullness of your calling. But God calls you to walk boldly, knowing that He has equipped you for everything He has placed before you.

Think of David before he became king. He was overlooked by his family, a simple shepherd boy who was out killing lions and bears and ultimately, taking out giants, underestimated by his entire family, including his own father, yet he had confidence in God. When he faced Goliath, he didn't rely on his own strength—he relied on God's power. He declared, "The Lord who rescued me from the paw of the lion and the paw of the bear will rescue me from the hand of this Philistine." (1 Samuel 17:37) David's confidence wasn't arrogance; it was trust in God's ability.

Self-Confidence vs. God-Confidence

There's a significant difference between self-confidence and God-confidence. Self-confidence is often built on shifting sands—achievements, appearances, abilities, or approval from others. When these foundations are shaken, so is your confidence.

Godly confidence, (God-fidence, as we referred to it before) however, is built on the unchanging character and nature of God. It's not about believing that you can do anything; it's about believing that God can do anything through you. Philippians 4:13 reminds us, "I can do all things through Christ who strengthens me." This verse isn't a blank check for any pursuit; it's a reminder that whatever God calls us to do, He also empowers us to accomplish. There is a saying that God gives you provision along with His vision.

Moses initially lacked confidence when God called him to lead Israel. He focused on his limitations, his speech impediment, his past failures, his inadequacies. God never asked Moses to rely on his own personal strengths and abilities. There was no assessment that he took to prove his abilities. He simply asked him to trust divine provision. God's response to Moses' insecurities was, "Who gave human beings their mouths?... Now go; I will help you speak and will teach you what to say." (Exodus 4:11-12) True confidence comes when we shift our focus from our limitations to God's limitless power.

The Root of Confidence Struggles

There are many reasons people struggle with confidence. It could be past experiences or failures, harsh words spoken over them, or the fear of making mistakes. Confidence is built when we recognize that our worth is not based on human opinions but on God's truth. When we align our thinking with God's promises; we develop an unshakable foundation.

The enemy often targets our confidence because he knows a confident believer is a dangerous threat to his kingdom of darkness. He uses several tactics:

1. **Comparison** - Getting us to measure ourselves against others always leads to either pride or despair

2. **Condemnation** - Keeping us focused on past failures rather than God's forgiveness

3. **Criticism** - Using the harsh words of others to define our worth

4. **Catastrophizing** - Magnifying potential failures to paralyze us with fear

Recognizing these tactics is the first step in developing resilient confidence. When we understand that these thoughts are not from God, we can reject them and choose to believe what God says about us instead.

Keys to Walking in Confidence

Walking in confidence means:

1. **Knowing Who You Are in Christ** – Your identity isn't based on achievements, looks, or status. It's rooted in God's love for you as expressed by Him giving His only begotten son. Still not sure who you are? Ephesians 1 outlines your spiritual identity—chosen, adopted, redeemed, forgiven, sealed with Holy Spirit. These truths don't change based on your performance.

2. **Rejecting Fear and Doubt** – Confidence comes from faith, not from perfect circumstances. 2 Timothy 1:7 reminds us, "For God has not given us a spirit of fear, but of power and of love and of a sound mind." When fear rises, recognize it as a signal to deepen your trust in God.

3. **Standing Firm in God's Promises** – What He has spoken over you is greater than what the enemy whispers. Joshua 1:9 declares, "Have I not commanded you? Be strong and courageous. Do not be afraid; do not be discouraged, for the LORD your God will be with you wherever you go." God's promises provide the bedrock for unshakable confidence.

4. **Taking Action** – Feel the fear and do it anyway. Confidence grows when you step out in faith despite your fears. Faith is not the absence of fear; it's moving forward despite it. Noah built an

ark before seeing rain. Abraham left his homeland before knowing the destination. Each step of obedience strengthens your confidence muscle.

5. **Embracing Imperfection** – Confidence isn't about being flawless; it's about trusting God's grace in your journey. Paul learned to boast in his weaknesses because they displayed God's strength (2 Corinthians 12:9). Perfectionism is the enemy of confidence because it sets an impossible standard.

6. **Speaking Life Over Yourself** – Words have power. Speak God's truth over your life daily. Proverbs 18:21 tells us, "The tongue has the power of life and death." Choose words that align with how God sees you, not how fear or insecurity might define you.

7. **Trusting the Process** – Confidence is built over time as we step out and see God move. Each experience of God's faithfulness becomes a stone of remembrance, like those the Israelites placed by the Jordan River (Joshua 4). These reminders of God's past faithfulness fuel confidence for future challenges.

The Journey of Confidence

Confidence isn't built overnight. Even biblical heroes experienced moments of doubt and fear. Abraham, called the father of faith, twice passed his wife off as his sister out of fear. Peter, bold enough to walk on water, later denied Jesus three times. Yet God didn't reject them for their lapses in confidence—He restored and strengthened them.

Your confidence will also grow through a process of steps and missteps, successes and failures, your challenges and victories. Each experience becomes part of your faith journey, teaching you to rely less on yourself and more on God's unfailing character.

Exiting Hell Moment

You are standing before a closed door, hesitant to turn the handle. Fear tells you to walk away, but God reminds you that He has already made a way. As you push forward with confidence, the door swings open, revealing a path of purpose and blessing. The path may not be easy, but you walk it with assurance, knowing that the One who called you is faithful to complete the work He has begun in you. (Philippians 1:6)

The hell of insecurity keeps you small, hiding your gifts and shrinking from opportunities. But God has called you to live boldly—not with pride or presumption, but with humble confidence in His ability to work through you. Step out of the shadows of self-doubt into the light of God's truth about who you are and what you're capable of through His strength. Doubt and insecurity can be paralyzing, keeping you in a personal prison. Today, make a choice to walk in the confidence God has given you. *Exhale* uncertainty and *inhale* divine assurance.

Affirmation

I am confident in the Lord, standing firm in the knowledge that He has fully equipped me for my divine calling. I walk boldly in faith, not trusting in my limited abilities but in the almighty God who works powerfully within me, transforming ordinary efforts into extraordinary outcomes through His unlimited strength and perfect wisdom.

Action Step/Journal Prompt

Write down three areas in your life where you need to walk in greater confidence. Then, find a Scripture to declare over each situation daily. Finally, identify one small action step you can take this week that requires confidence—something that stretches your faith but is achievable with God's help. Record how you feel before taking that step and how you feel afterward, noting how God met you in that moment of faith.

BONUS
Confidence in Community

God often builds our confidence through community. Sometimes we need others to believe in us before we can believe in ourselves. Barnabas (whose name means "son of encouragement") stood by Paul when others doubted his conversion. His confidence in Paul helped the early church trust Paul's transformation.

Similarly, in 1 Samuel 23:16, "Jonathan, Saul's son, went to David at Horesh and helped him find strength in God." In moments when David's confidence may have faltered, Jonathan was there to remind him of God's promises.

Who are the confidence-builders in your life? Who reminds you of God's promises when you forget? And for whom might you be a "Barnabas" or "Jonathan," helping them find strength in God when their confidence wavers?

Don't have anyone? You are welcome to join WOW Ministries Global! We are a community of believers that have been known to pray not just with our words, but also with our feet. Every single day, we pray for one another and for everyone that has ever connected with us. For more details, visit www.WOWMinistriesGlobal.org and get connected to WOW, a safe community for you to grow into your God-breathed purpose.

Day 18: No Battle? No Victory.

Scripture Focus

"The Lord will fight for you; you need only to be still." — Exodus 14:14 (NIV)

Reflection

There are moments in life when we feel overwhelmed by the battles we face. Whether it's a struggle with fear, doubt, financial hardships, broken relationships, or emotional wounds, the weight can feel unbearable. We try to fight on our own, exhausting ourselves in the process, forgetting that we were never meant to carry these burdens alone.

You cannot have victory without a battle. 1 Corinthians 15:57 (NIV) says, "But thanks be to God! He gives us the victory through our Lord Jesus Christ." This Scripture makes an astounding promise. God always leads us to triumph or victory! It may seem obvious, but the fact remains that in order to have victory, you must be in a battle. The promise is not that we will walk in a constant state of victoriousness, but rather that in every situation, God will lead us in triumph. We can't even say we will always know what victory will look like. Only that victory is the Lord's irrevocable promise. True faith will stand on this promise in the face of every trial, challenge, or opposition, remembering that the greatest purpose of every victory is manifesting the fragrance of our knowledge of Him.

God's Pattern of Victory

The Israelites faced an impossible situation when they stood before the Red Sea with Pharaoh's army pursuing them. Fear gripped their hearts, and they questioned why they had ever left Egypt. Yet in that moment, Moses spoke words of faith: "The Lord will fight for you; you need only to be still." And then, God did the impossible—He parted the sea, making a way where there was none.

It's easy to feel like we have to fight our own battles. Society often tells us that we need to be strong, independent, and in control of every situation. We internalize this message, believing that asking for help is a sign of weakness. But in reality, the greatest strength comes from surrendering to God. When we let go and allow Him to fight for us, we access divine power far greater than anything we could muster on our own.

Learning from Jehoshaphat

Consider the story of Jehoshaphat in 2 Chronicles 20. When faced with a vast enemy army, he didn't immediately prepare for war; instead, he sought the Lord. He declared a fast throughout Judah and prayed, saying, "We do not know what to do, but our eyes are upon you." (2 Chronicles 20:12). God's response? "Do not be afraid or discouraged because of this vast army. For the battle is not yours, but God's" (2 Chronicles 20:15). Jehoshaphat responded in faith, and instead of sending warriors to the front lines, he sent worshippers. As they praised God, their enemies turned on each other, and Judah won the battle without ever lifting a sword.

What battles are you trying to fight on your own? Have you been struggling to fix a relationship, control an outcome, or carry a burden that isn't yours to bear? God is calling you to lay it down and trust Him. He never intended for you to fight alone.

The Surrender of Control

When we try to control everything, we get in the way of God's plan. Proverbs 16:9 says that "man plans, but God directs." Surrendering doesn't mean giving up—it means acknowledging that God is greater, wiser, and stronger than we are. It means trusting that He has already worked it out, even when we don't see immediate results.

Imagine a child trying to carry a heavy suitcase while their father stands beside them, waiting to help. The child struggles, refusing to let go, insisting they can do it alone. But the moment they surrender and allow their father to take the burden, they find relief. This is how God waits for us. He is willing to carry the weight, but He won't force it out of our hands—we must willingly place it in His.

Perhaps your battle is emotional—a deep wound from your past that you keep revisiting. You try to heal yourself, to make sense of it all, but the pain lingers. Or maybe you're dealing with financial struggles, wondering how you'll make ends meet, constantly striving, worrying, and pushing forward in your own strength. God is saying, "Be still. Let Me fight for you."

Practical Steps to Victory

Here's how you can start letting God fight your battles:

1. **Acknowledge the Battle** – Identify what is troubling your heart, weighing on your mind, or causing spiritual heaviness. Bring it to God in prayer with honesty and humility, knowing that He cares for every detail. Writing it down becomes a prophetic act of surrender—physically releasing what you were never meant to carry alone.

2. **Declare God's Promises** – Open your mouth and declare God's Word over your life—His promises are your legal rights as His child. Scriptures like *Exodus 14:14*, "The Lord will fight for you," and *Romans 8:28*, "All things work together for good," are not just encouragements, they are divine truths. Meditate daily on these promises until your heart aligns with Heaven's perspective.

3. **Step back in faith** – Stepping back doesn't mean giving up—it means trusting God to do what only He can. Faith is active, even in waiting, so keep walking in obedience even when the breakthrough hasn't come. Your role is to move forward with trust, not to manipulate the outcome.

4. **Pray and praise** – Prayer connects you to God's heart, and praise anchors you in His power. Worship isn't a filler—it's a force that breaks chains, calms storms, and shifts atmospheres. When you lift your voice in praise, your spirit rises above the battle and aligns with victory.

5. **Refuse to pick the battle back up** – Once you've surrendered something to God, resist the urge to worry, micromanage, or replay it in your mind. Trust that He is working behind the scenes, even when you can't see it. Choosing peace is not passive; it's a bold declaration that God is still in control.

God's Unexpected Battle Plans

The reality is that many of the battles we fight are spiritual. Ephesians 6:12 reminds us, "For our struggle is not against flesh and blood, but against the rulers, against the authorities, against the powers of this dark world and against the spiritual forces of evil in the heavenly realms." The enemy wants to keep you trapped in fear, doubt, and exhaustion. But when you let God take over, you walk in victory.

Sometimes, trusting God's battle plan doesn't make sense in the natural. When God told the Israelites to march around Jericho for seven days instead of attacking it, it must have seemed absurd. But their obedience led to a supernatural victory. When God told Gideon to reduce his army from 32,000 men to just 300, it must have seemed like a guaranteed loss. But
God used that small army to defeat the Midianites, proving that the battle belongs to Him.

Imagine this: You are standing on the battlefield, exhausted and weary. Then, you hear God's voice saying, "Step aside, My child. I've got this." You drop your sword, step back, and watch as God moves in ways you never imagined. Victory was never about your strength—it was always about His.

Your obedience guarantees your victory.

Day 18: No Battle? No Victory.

Exiting Hell Moment

Trying to fight battles on your own is its own form of torment. It leads to exhaustion, frustration, and despair. But God is calling you to release the fight to Him. Today, choose to step back, trust Him, and watch Him work. *Exhale* anxiety and *inhale* divine peace.

Affirmation

I trust God to fight my battles with perfect wisdom and sovereign power that far exceeds my own strength or strategy. I am not alone in my struggles, for the Creator of the universe stands beside me, working all things together for my ultimate good and ensuring that victory already belongs to Him before the battle even begins.

Action Step/Journal Prompt

Write down one battle you have been fighting on your own. Now, write a surrender prayer, releasing it to God. Keep this prayer somewhere visible as a reminder that the battle is His, not yours.

Day 19: Breaking Chains and Moving Forward

Scripture Focus

"Therefore if the Son make you free, you shall be free indeed." — John 8:36

Reflection

Many people live in invisible chains, most are based in the fear of something—fear of failure, fear of rejection, shame from past sins, negative mindsets, or feeling unworthy of God's love. These chains keep them bound even though Christ has already declared them free. The key to breaking free is surrendering those burdens fully to God and refusing to pick them back up.

Consider Paul and Silas in Acts 16. They were imprisoned, chained, and yet they worshiped. As they praised God, an earthquake shook the prison, their chains fell off, and the doors swung open. Their physical freedom mirrored the spiritual freedom that comes when we choose to trust God fully.

Breaking free from the things that have held you back is a process. Today is the day to step fully into the freedom God has for you.

Understanding True Freedom

Freedom in Christ is different from the world's definition of freedom. The world often defines freedom as the ability to do whatever you want without restraint. Biblical freedom is not just a license—it's liberation with purpose. It's being set free from bondage to sin and death so that you can live abundantly as God intended.

The enemy wants to keep you bound in chains that limit your potential and purpose. Christ wants to break those chains so you can experience the fullness of life in Him. Jesus said in John 10:10 (NIV), "The thief comes only to steal and kill and destroy; I have come that they may have life and have it to the full."

True freedom isn't just about what you're freed from, it's about what you're freed for. You're not just liberated from sin; you're liberated for service, for love, for purpose, for intimacy with God. Galatians 5:13 reminds us, "For, brethren, ye have been called unto liberty; only use not liberty for an occasion to the flesh, but by love serve one another." It's important that you do not use your freedom to indulge the flesh; rather, serve one another humbly in love.

The Chains That Bind Us

The chains that bind us come in many forms. Often, they share common roots:

1. **Past Trauma** can lock us in defensive patterns that may have once protected us but now limit us. Like the Israelites who longed for Egypt's familiarity even after God freed them from slavery, we sometimes cling to old pain because it's what we know.

2. **Unforgiveness** binds both the forgiver and the forgiven. When we withhold forgiveness, we remain chained to the very person or situation that hurt us. As Holocaust survivor Corrie ten Boom said, "Forgiveness is setting the prisoner free, only to discover the prisoner was you."

3. **False Identity** forms chains when we believe lies about who we are rather than embracing our identity in Christ. The enemy whispers, "You are what you've done" or "You are what was done to you." God declares, "You are who I say you are—beloved, redeemed, and purposed."

Day 19: Breaking Chains and Moving Forward

4. **Fear**, that dreaded 4-letter word, paralyzes and confines us to small, safe spaces rather than the wide-open freedom God intends. It manifests as anxiety about the future, dread of failure, or terror of rejection. Yet 1 John 4:18 reminds us that "perfect love drives out fear."

5. **Unhealthy Attachments** to people, substances, or behaviors can become chains that promise comfort but deliver bondage. These attachments often serve as counterfeit sources of love, value, or security that only God can truly provide.

6. **Religious Legalism** creates chains of performance, measuring worth by adherence to rules rather than relationship with Christ. This was the yoke Jesus referenced when He invited, "Come to me, all you who are weary and burdened, and I will give you rest" (Matthew 11:28).

Biblical Examples of Breaking Free

Through Scripture, we see powerful examples of people who experienced freedom from various forms of bondage:

1. **The Woman Caught in Adultery** (John 8:1-11) faced public shame and a death sentence. Jesus dispersed her accusers and declared, "Neither do I condemn you; go, and from now on sin no more." He broke the chains of both condemnation and sin in her life.

2. **The Apostle Peter** was imprisoned both literally (Acts 12) and by his own fear and denial (John 18). Yet God freed him from physical chains through an angel, and from the chains of shame through Christ's restoration (John 21). The man who once denied Jesus three times became a bold witness, even unto death.

3. **The Prodigal Son** (Luke 15:11-32) was bound by the chains of his own rebellion and poor choices. In his moment of clarity, he returned home expecting servitude but received sonship instead. His father's embrace broke the chains of shame and unworthiness.

The Path to True Freedom

True freedom requires:

1. **Letting Go of the Past** – You can't move forward while holding onto chains from yesterday. Isaiah 43:18-19 encourages, "Forget the former things; do not dwell on the past. See, I am doing a new thing!" Your history simply tells your story. It doesn't have to determine your destiny.

2. **Forgiving Yourself and Others** – Forgiveness releases you from the bondage of bitterness and regret. It doesn't excuse the wrong but breaks its power over you. Forgiveness may need to be a daily choice before it becomes a settled reality in your heart.

3. **Trusting God's Plan** – His ways are higher, and His freedom is complete. Proverbs 3:5-6 reminds us to "Trust in the LORD with all your heart and lean not on your own understanding; in all your ways submit to him, and he will make your paths straight." Freedom flourishes in the soil of surrender.

4. **Walking in Obedience** – Freedom isn't just about release; it's about stepping into a new way of living. John 8:31-32 says, "If you hold to my teaching, you are really my disciples. Then you will know the truth, and the truth will set you free." Obedience to God's Word isn't restriction—it's protection and direction.

5. **Declaring Victory Daily** – Your words have power. Speak freedom over your life. Romans 10:10 tells us, "For it is with your heart that you believe and are justified, and it is with your

Mouth that you profess your faith and are saved." What you consistently declare shapes what you ultimately believe.

6. **Releasing the Lies of the Enemy** – The devil will try to convince you that you are still bound. Choose to believe God's truth instead. 2 Corinthians 10:5 instructs us to "take captive every thought to make it obedient to Christ." Freedom begins in the battlefield of the mind.

7. **Living in Gratitude** – Celebrate every step of progress in your journey to freedom. Philippians 4:6-7 encourages, "Do not be anxious about anything, but in every situation, by prayer and petition, with thanksgiving, present your requests to God." Gratitude shifts your focus from what still binds you to how far God has brought you.

The Process of Breaking Chains

Breaking free is rarely instantaneous. Typically, it's a process that unfolds over time. Just as the Israelites had to journey through the wilderness after their liberation from Egypt, your path to complete freedom may include wilderness seasons. These periods aren't detours; they're necessary parts of your transformation. The process often includes:

Awareness – Recognizing the chains that bind you. Some chains are obvious; others are subtle, disguised as protection or even virtue. Ask God to reveal what's holding you back.

Acknowledgment – Admitting the impact these chains have had on your life and relationships. This requires honesty with yourself, God, and often with trusted others.

Repentance – Turning away from patterns that have kept your bound. Repentance isn't just feeling sorry; it's changing direction.

Replacement – Filling the void left by broken chains with God's truth, healthy relationships, and new patterns of thinking and living.

Persistence – Continuing forward even when old patterns try to reassert themselves. Freedom is maintained through vigilance and continued surrender to God.

Community's Role in Freedom

God rarely sets us free in isolation. He uses community—the body of Christ—as an instrument of liberation and support. Galatians 6:2 instructs us to "Carry each other's burdens, and in this way, you will fulfill the law of Christ."

The paralyzed man couldn't reach Jesus on his own, his four friends tore through the roof to lower him to Christ (Mark 2:1-12). We always talk about the man that was healed. Were it not for his friends, he may never have had that experience. We all need friends who believe in your freedom enough to tear off roofs and break barriers.

James 5:16 encourages, "Therefore confess your sins to each other and pray for each other so that you may be healed." There is healing power in bringing struggles into the light of a trusted community rather than battling alone in darkness.

Exiting Hell Moment

Remaining in bondage to past struggles is its own version of hell. But today, claim the freedom Christ has already given you. *Exhale* captivity and *inhale* liberty.

The prison of your past has no authority to determine your future. The cell door has been unlocked by Christ's sacrifice. The chains have been broken by His resurrection power. All that remains is for you to walk out into the freedom He has already secured. Step out of the shadows of bondage into the light of liberation, where you can breathe deeply of grace and move freely in purpose.

Affirmation

I am free in Christ, completely liberated from the chains that once held me captive to my past mistakes and limiting beliefs. I let go of what was and move forward in victory, knowing that what once bound me no longer defines me because I now walk confidently in the precious freedom that was purchased for me at the cross of Calvary.

Action Step/Journal Prompt

Write down one thing that has been holding you back from living in true freedom. Pray over it and make a commitment to release it to God today. Then, identify one practical step you can take this week to walk in freedom in this area. Finally, ask yourself, who could help support me in my journey to freedom? Reach out to that person and share your commitment to breaking free from what has held you back.

Day 20: Enter God's Rest

Scripture Focus

"Come to me, all who labor and are heavy laden, and I will give you rest."
— *Matthew 11:28 ESV*

Reflection

As women, we tend to nurture everyone around us other than ourselves. We take care of everyone: kids, family, friends, coworkers, and whoever else we encounter. We make sure they have everything they need, regardless of whether or not we are getting what we need. We brag about our ability to do more with less – to multitask even. We don't realize there is no such thing. We are simply shifting our thoughts back and forth very quickly. This is exhausting and it causes us to operate less than optimally.

Now that you know you are the prize, it is time to treat yourself like the prize. Step out of your box and do something for yourself you never imagined you would do.

The Biblical Foundation for Self-Care

God's invitation to rest is not just a suggestion—it's a divine principle woven throughout Scripture. From the creation account where God rested on the seventh day, to Jesus' invitation in Matthew 11:28, the Bible consistently affirms the importance of rest and renewal.

Proper stewardship demands that we diligently take care of that which we have been blessed with – even our own bodies. You cannot give from an empty vessel. Caring for yourself is not just about personal wellness—it's about honoring the temple God has given you. 1 Corinthians 6:19-20 reminds us that our bodies are temples of the Holy Spirit, and we are called to glorify God in our bodies.

The command to "love your neighbor as yourself" (Leviticus 19:18) assumes that you already love yourself. As the passage states, you are to love your neighbor as yourself. How can you properly love another person when you don't love yourself? This principle establishes that healthy love of self is the foundation for loving others well.

Scripture further affirms this in Ephesians 5:29: "For no man ever hated his own flesh but nourishes and carefully protects and cherishes it." The natural order is to care for ourselves—to nourish, protect, and cherish our own wellbeing—not out of selfishness but as part of God's design.

Understanding Sabbath Rest

The concept of Sabbath originated in Genesis when God rested on the seventh day, not because He was tired, but to establish a pattern for humanity. This pattern was later codified in the Ten Commandments: "Remember the sabbath day, to keep it holy." (Exodus 20:8)

Sabbath is more than just a day of the week—it's a principle of regular, intentional rest that acknowledges our human limitations and our dependence on God. Jesus clarified the purpose of Sabbath when He said, "The Sabbath was made for man, not man for the Sabbath" (Mark 2:27). It exists for our benefit, not as a burdensome rule.

In our 24/7 culture, Sabbath may seem like an ancient, irrelevant practice. Yet its principles are more necessary than ever. Constant connectivity, endless to-do lists, and the blur between work and home life leave many women exhausted and depleted. Sabbath offers a counter-cultural rhythm that says, "Stop. Rest. Remember who you are and whose you are."

Entering Sabbath Rest

How do we practically enter into Sabbath rest in today's busy world? Here are some principles to guide you:

1. **Set Aside Dedicated Time** – Whether it's a traditional Sabbath day or another time that works for your schedule, intentionally carve out regular, uninterrupted time for rest and renewal. This might be a full day, a half-day, or even a few sacred hours each week.

2. **Cease from Work** – True Sabbath involves stopping your normal work and productivity. This doesn't just mean paid employment, but also household tasks, errands, and the mental labor of planning and problem-solving. Give yourself permission to lay these burdens down temporarily.

3. **Disconnect to Reconnect** – Consider a technology fast during your Sabbath time. Put away phones, computers, and other devices that constantly demand your attention. This creates space to be fully present with yourself, your loved ones, and God.

4. **Engage in Life-Giving Activities** – Sabbath isn't just about what you don't do; it's about what you do. Fill this time with activities that restore your soul—perhaps reading, walking in nature, enjoying unhurried conversations, creating art, or simply sitting in silence.

5. **Practice Gratitude and Worship** – Sabbath is a time to shift from producing to praising, from acquiring to appreciating. Take time to acknowledge God's goodness and provision in your life. This might include formal worship or simply cultivating an attitude of thankfulness.

6. **Rest Your Body** – Physical rest is an essential component of Sabbath. Allow yourself to sleep in, take a nap, move your body in gentle ways, or simply sit still without guilt.

7. **Feast and Celebrate** – Many Sabbath traditions include special meals or treats. This celebrates God's abundance and reminds us that rest isn't merely utilitarian—it's meant to be enjoyed.

Remember that Sabbath practices may look different depending on your life season, family situation, and personal needs. A young mother with small children will practice Sabbath differently than a woman living alone or someone caring for aging parents. The external forms may vary, but the principles remain the same ceasing from labor, delighting in God's gifts, and remembering who you are in Him.

Breaking Out of Unhealthy Patterns

When we neglect self-care and Sabbath rest, we often find ourselves in unhealthy relationships and situations. An imbalance in self-care "creates an imbalance and attracts people who want to use and not 'add value' to your life and space." Learning to value yourself is not just for your benefit—it helps establish healthy boundaries that lead to more fulfilling relationships.

Many of us have been conditioned to believe that putting ourselves last is virtuous. While selflessness is certainly a Christian value, neglecting your own legitimate needs is not what God intends. Jesus Himself withdrew regularly to pray and rest (Luke 5:16), thereby modeling the rhythm of engagement and renewal that sustains ministry and relationships.

The Spiritual Dimension of Rest

Rest is more than physical relaxation—it's a spiritual posture. Hebrews 4 speaks of entering God's rest through faith. This rest is both a present reality and a future promise, a ceasing from our own works and a trusting in God's completed work.

This deeper spiritual rest comes from surrendering our striving and trusting in God's sufficiency. It's the rest that remains available to God's people (Hebrews 4:9)—a soul-level peace that transcends circumstances. We enter this rest by believing in God's promises, releasing our grip on control, and receiving His grace.

Spiritual rest also involves resting from worry, fear, and the need to fix everything. Jesus invites us to cast our anxieties on Him (1 Peter 5:7) and to exchange our burdens for His lighter yoke (Matthew 11:28-30). This exchange happens as we practice the spiritual disciplines of prayer, meditation on Scripture, silence, and solitude.

When Jesus invites the weary and burdened to come to Him for rest in Matthew 11:28, He follows this with an invitation to take His yoke and lean on Him. This teaches us that true rest isn't about absence of activity but about alignment with God's purposes and rhythms.

Practical Steps for Self-Care

Step out of your comfort zone. This doesn't have to be a major act. Take baby steps:

1. **Be Aware of Your Own Self-Talk** – Counteract negative self-talk with what God says about you. Replace thoughts like "I'm not enough" with truths like "I am fearfully and wonderfully made" (Psalm 139:14).

2. **Learn to Say No** – You don't have to be everything to everyone. Give yourself permission to say "No". Boundaries are biblical; even Jesus set limits on what He would do and with whom He would do it.

3. **Use Positive Affirmations** – Remind yourself who you are on a daily basis. Now say it until you believe it. Speak God's promises over your life until they sink from your head to your heart.

4. **Decide to 'Like' Yourself** – In other words, choose you. Be your own best friend. You can't love yourself until you like yourself. Consider your own positive qualities and the unique gifts God has given you.

Adding Value to Your Life

This devotion encourages you to add value to your life, eat healthy, get 6-8 hours of sleep. Spend time on yourself. These practical aspects of self-care honor God by stewarding the resources He's given you:

- **Physical Care**: Your body needs proper nutrition, adequate sleep, and regular movement. These aren't luxuries but necessities for health and vitality.

- **Emotional Care**: Processing feelings, establishing boundaries, and nurturing healthy relationships all contribute to emotional wellbeing.

- **Mental Care**: Stimulating your mind, learning new things, and challenging negative thought patterns renew your mind. (Romans 12:2).

- **Spiritual Care**: Time in God's Word, prayer, worship, and community grounds you in your true identity and purpose.

When you prioritize these aspects of self-care, you're better equipped to fulfill your calling and love others well. You're not being selfish—you're being a good steward of what God has entrusted to you.

Rhythms of Rest and Renewal

God designed all of creation to function according to rhythms—day and night, seasons, tides, heartbeats. Human beings are no exception. We need regular patterns of work and rest, engagement and withdrawal, activity and renewal.

Consider implementing these rhythms in your life:

- **Daily**: Take short pauses throughout your day—perhaps a few minutes of quiet reflection in the morning, a midday break to breathe deeply and reconnect with God, or an evening ritual that helps you transition from activity to rest.

- **Weekly**: Set aside your Sabbath time—whether a traditional day of rest or another arrangement that works for your life season. Guard this time carefully against encroachment.

- **Seasonally**: Pay attention to the different seasons of your life. Some periods require more intense activity; others allow for more spaciousness. Honor these rhythms rather than expecting consistent productivity.

- **Annually**: Many spiritual traditions include annual retreats or extended periods of rest. Consider planning a personal retreat day or weekend once or twice a year for deeper renewal.

These rhythms aren't rigid rules but flexible practices that help you remain in sync with God's design for human flourishing. They create a sustainable pattern that prevents burnout and nurtures lasting joy.

Overcoming Guilt About Self-Care

Many women struggle with guilt when they take time for themselves. If this describes you, remember that Jesus Himself took time away from ministry to rest. He withdrew from crowds, spent time in prayer, and even slept during a storm. His example gives us permission to rest without guilt.

Some common guilt-inducing thoughts and their counterarguments:

- **"Others need me too much for me to rest."** Counter-thought: "I can serve others better when I'm rested and renewed."

- **"I'm being selfish if I take time for myself."** Counter-thought: "Self-care is stewardship, not selfishness. I'm honoring God by caring for His temple."

- **"I should be productive all the time."** Counter-thought: "Even God rested. My value isn't in my productivity but in my identity as His beloved."

- **"I don't deserve to rest until everything is done."** Counterthought: "The work will never be completely done. Rest is a gift to receive, not a reward to earn."

Rest and self-care aren't optional extras for when everything else is done. They're essential components of a healthy, God-honoring life. As you learn to value yourself as God values you, you'll find greater capacity to love and serve others from a place of fullness rather than depletion.

Exiting Hell Moment

There's an old saying inspired by a teacup and saucer: *"I'm drinking from my saucer because my cup has overflowed."* Imagine yourself as the teacup—your time, energy, love, wisdom, and strength are all held within that cup. That cup sits in a saucer. The saucer is there to collect the overflow. You were never to pour out of your cup. Rather, you are to pour out of the saucer – to give from the overflow.

God never asked us to give from depletion. He desires for us to be filled first—filled with His Spirit, His Word, His peace, and His purpose—so that what we give to others flows from the abundance He provides, not from our own survival. When you pour from the saucer, you're giving from the overflow—no resentment, no burnout, just a generous outpouring from a soul that's already full.

Check your cup. Are you giving from what you have, or from the overflow that He gave? Stay filled. Stay rooted. Let Him fill you daily—so that what spills out blesses others without emptying you. That's Kingdom stewardship. That's living and giving from the overflow.

Day 20: Enter God's Rest

The hell of constant self-neglect leaves you exhausted, resentful, and unable to fully experience or extend God's love. Today, step out of the prison of endless doing into the freedom of being—being loved, being valued, being enough in Christ.

Take a deep breath and *exhale* the pressure to be all things to all people. *Inhale* the grace to be who God created you to be, including the grace to rest and receive. The door to this prison has always been unlocked. Christ opened it through His finished work. You need only walk through it into the spacious place of Sabbath rest that awaits you.

Affirmation

I am worthy of care and rest, embracing God's divine rhythm of Sabbath not as a luxury but as a sacred necessity for my soul's flourishing. I nurture myself with intentional self-care, honoring my Creator who designed renewal as essential to my purpose, and becoming more abundantly equipped to pour out authentic love to others from my replenished wellspring.

Action Step/Journal Prompt

Today, take 15 minutes and do something specifically for yourself. Go for a walk, browse a bookstore, enjoy a cup of tea in silence or something else that you enjoy. Don't feel guilty; you deserve it.

Then, plan a more extended Sabbath experience for this week. What day or part of a day can you set aside? What will you stop doing during this time? What life-giving activities will you include? How will you connect with God during this time? Write down your Sabbath plan and commit to following through, noticing how this practice affects your overall wellbeing.

Phase 3: Empowerment and Moving Forward (Days 21-31)

Day 21: Overcoming Fear with Faith

Scripture Focus

"For God hath not given us the spirit of fear, but of power, and of love, and of a sound mind." — 2 Timothy 1:7

Reflection

Fear is one of the most powerful emotions that can hold us captive. It whispers lies, telling us we are not capable, not worthy, and not strong enough. It paralyzes us, keeping us stuck in cycles of doubt and insecurity. Fear is not from God. He has given us power, love, and a sound mind—tools to overcome fear and walk boldly in faith.

Joshua, was tasked with leading the Israelites into the Promised Land after Moses' death. The journey ahead was filled with uncertainty and challenges, but God told him, "Have not I commanded thee? Be strong and of a good courageous; be not afraid, neither be thou dismayed: for the Lord your God is with thee whithersoever thou goest." (Joshua 1:9). This is one of my favorite Scriptures in the entire Bible. Joshua had every reason to fear, but he chose faith instead. Because of his obedience, the Israelites saw victory after victory.

The Disguise of Fear

Fear often disguises itself as wisdom. It convinces us that playing it safe, that playing it small, is better than taking risks and playing full out. It tells us that avoiding failure is more important than pursuing God's purpose. True wisdom comes from trusting God, not from allowing fear to dictate our decisions. Fear will always try to keep you in a box. Faith calls you to step out and trust God with the unknown.

Have you ever been afraid to start a new chapter in life—maybe it's a new career, a new relationship, or a move to a different place? The fear of the unknown can be overwhelming, paralyzing even. When we choose to trust God's plan, we realize that He has gone before us and prepared the way. When I left my job, decades ago, my mother was so afraid for me. "How could you leave such a beautiful building?" she would ask. She worried about financial stability, about how I would take care of my children, about whether I was truly capable of stepping successfully into entrepreneurship. She and Dad only knew of one way to succeed. I'm sure you've heard the formula for yourself: go to school, get a good job and retire with a pension, rather than your passion. I took a leap of faith. Not only did I find a better job, I not only found peace, growth, and a deeper trust in God, but I also created more income than I ever would have hoped for working for someone else.

The Root of Our Fears

To truly overcome fear, we must understand its origin. Most of our fears stem from one of three sources:

1. **Past trauma or Failures** - Negative experiences, ours or others, can leave deep imprints on our hearts and minds, causing us to fear similar situations.

2. **Uncertainty about the Future** - The unknown can be terrifying because we cannot control it or predict its outcomes.

3. **False beliefs about Ourselves or God** - When we don't fully grasp our identity in Christ or the nature of God's character, fear finds fertile ground.

The enemy uses these roots to cultivate fear in our lives. He knows that a fearful Christian is an ineffective Christian. 1 John 4:18 reminds us that "perfect love casts out all fear." When we immerse ourselves in God's perfect love, recognizing His sovereignty and receiving His goodness, fear loses its grip.

Biblical Examples of Faith Over Fear

The Bible is filled with examples of people who faced tremendous fears yet chose faith:

> David faced the giant Goliath when seasoned warriors would not. He approached the battle not with fear but with confidence in God's power, declaring, "The battle is the Lord's" (1 Samuel 17:47).

> Esther risked her life by approaching the king uninvited to save her people. Her famous words, "If I perish, I perish" (Esther 4:16), demonstrate a willingness to move forward despite fear of death.

> The disciples feared for their lives during a violent storm, while Jesus slept peacefully in the boat. When they woke Him in panic, He calmed both the storm outside and the storm of fear within them, asking, "Why are you so afraid? Do you still have no faith?" (Mark 4:40). Those same disciples were frightened when they encountered Jesus in the Upper Room.

These examples teach us that faith is not the absence of danger but the presence of trust in a God who is greater than any threat we face.

Breaking Free from Fear's Grip

What is fear keeping you from today? Is it stopping you from pursuing a dream? From healing a broken relationship? From stepping into a calling God has placed on your heart? Fear is both a magnet and a magnifier. It attracts and magnifies problems, making them seem impossible to overcome. But faith shifts your perspective, reminding you that nothing is impossible for God.

Steps to Overcome Fear with Faith

Here are some steps to overcome fear with faith:

1. **Acknowledge your Fear** – Denying it won't make it go away. Identify what you are afraid of and bring it before God.

2. **Pray for Courage** – Ask God to strengthen your faith and help you trust Him in the face of uncertainty.

3. **Feel the Fear and Do it Anyway**– Courage isn't the absence of fear; it's moving forward in faith despite feeling afraid.

4. **Meditate on God's Word** – Scriptures like 2 Timothy 1:7 and Isaiah 41:10 remind us of God's presence and power.

5. **Surround yourself with Faith-filled People** – Find those who will encourage you, pray for you, and remind you of God's promises. When I left my job, it was the inspiration of a few friends and business partners who made similar decisions and leaps of faith. Your friends are either driving you forward or holding you backward. Check them out. It's okay to admit that you need some new friends.

The Transformation of Fear

When we face our fears with faith, something remarkable happens. Those very fears can become catalysts for spiritual growth. What once paralyzed us becomes a platform for experiencing God's faithfulness. Every fear conquered becomes a testimony of God's power working in our lives.

Remember that God does not always remove the object of our fear. Sometimes, He chooses to walk with us through it, transforming us in the process. The three Hebrew young men — Shadrach, Meshach, and

Abednego—weren't delivered from the fiery furnace; they were delivered in it. God joined them in the flames, and they emerged unharmed and unbound. (Daniel 3:25-27)

This is often how God works in our lives. He doesn't always remove the fire, but He always joins us in it. When we walk with Him through our fears, we discover a depth of faith and intimacy with God that we couldn't have gained any other way.

Exiting Hell Moment

You are standing on the edge of a cliff, looking at a bridge that leads to the other side. Fear tells you the bridge won't hold. But then, you see God standing in the middle, extending His hand. He says, *"Trust Me."* You take a deep breath, step forward, and find that the bridge is stronger than you imagined. That is what faith does—it carries you where fear says you cannot go.

When you feel that familiar grip of fear tightening around your heart, remember that you have been given "power, love, and a sound mind." Power to face challenges, love to overcome habits of self-preservation, and a sound mind to discern truth from lies. You are stepping out of the prison of fear into the wide-open spaces of faith, where possibilities are limitless and His presence is assured.

Fear is a prison that keeps you from living the life God intended. Today, choose faith over fear. Step out, knowing that God is with you. **Exhale** doubt and ***inhale*** courage.

Affirmation

I am not ruled by fear that seeks to paralyze my potential and distort my perspective. I choose faith with unwavering conviction, standing firmly on the truth that God has given me power to overcome, love that casts out all fear, and a sound mind that remains anchored in His unchanging promises regardless of what circumstances might suggest.

Action Step/Journal Prompt

Write down one fear that has been holding you back. Then, write a declaration of faith to replace that fear. Speak it over yourself daily and pray for God's strength to walk in boldness. Finally, identify one small step you can take this week to act in faith despite this fear.

Day 22: Stepping Into Your Purpose

Scripture Focus

"For we are God's handiwork, created in Christ Jesus to do good works, which God prepared in advance for us to do." — Ephesians 2:10 (NIV)

Reflection

One of the greatest tragedies in life is not living out the purpose God has for you. Many people wander through life, unsure of why they were created or whether they have anything meaningful to contribute. Truth is, God designed you with a specific purpose in mind. Regardless of the circumstances of your birth, you are not here by accident, nor are you an accident.

Moses surely thought God had made a mistake when he was called God to lead the Israelites out of Egypt. He didn't just doubt his ability to lead, Moses couldn't speak without stuttering. He questioned whether he was the right person for the job. Despite his fears and excuses, God equipped him for the task ahead. Like Moses, you may feel inadequate or uncertain. Know that if God has called you, He has also equipped you with unique gifts and talents for the journey.

Stepping into your purpose requires faith, obedience, and a willingness to trust God's timing. Sometimes, we allow fear to hold us back and live as a 'wandering generality' when God intended for you to live as a 'destiny specific'. We fear failure, rejection, or stepping outside our comfort zones. Purpose is found on the other side of fear.

Understanding Divine Purpose

Purpose is as much about what you do as it is about who you are becoming. God's purpose for your life encompasses your character development as much as your actions. Romans 8:29 tells us that God predestined us to be conformed to the image of His Son. This transformation is a central aspect of your purpose.

Your purpose is also relational. You were created for communion with God and connection with others. The two greatest commandments—to love God and love your neighbor (Matthew 22:37-39)—form the foundation of your purpose. Whatever specific calling God has for your life will build upon these fundamental relationships.

Purpose is both universal and unique. All believers share the universal purposes of glorifying God, growing in Christlikeness, and participating in the Great Commission. Yet within these broader purposes, God has given each person unique gifts, passions, experiences, and opportunities that shape their individual calling.

Learning from Biblical Examples

Joseph walked into his God-ordained purpose despite hardship. He was sold into slavery by his own brothers, falsely accused, and imprisoned. Yet even in difficult seasons, Joseph remained faithful. In the end, God positioned him in a place of authority to save an entire nation from famine. The journey to your purpose may not always be smooth, but it is always worth it.

Consider Esther, who was placed in the royal palace "for such a time as this" (Esther 4:14). Her position of influence wasn't coincidental, it was providential. God had strategically positioned her to save her people from destruction. Like Esther, your current circumstances, relationships, and position, may be intentionally arranged by God as part of His purpose for your life.

David was an anointed king long before he took the throne. During the waiting period, he developed character, leadership skills, and intimate communion with God. His psalms reveal a man after God's own heart, formed through both victories and valleys. Your purpose often unfolds gradually, with each season building upon the last.

Nehemiah's purpose emerged from his burden for Jerusalem's broken walls. His grief moved him to action, and his practical leadership skills made him the perfect person to lead the rebuilding effort. Your deepest burdens and strongest compassions often point toward your purpose. What breaks your heart will usually reveal where God is calling you to make a difference.

Obstacles to Finding Your Purpose

Several common obstacles can prevent us from stepping fully into our purpose:

> **Comparison** derails purpose by fixing our eyes on someone else's journey rather than our own. When we compare, we either feel inadequate (if we perceive others as more successful) or complacent (if we perceive ourselves as ahead). Either way, comparison distracts us from the unique path God has for us.
>
> **Past Failures** can convince us we're disqualified from meaningful purpose. Yet Scripture is filled with flawed individuals whom God used powerfully. Peter denied Christ three times but became a foundational leader in the early church. Your failures don't disqualify you; often, they prepare you.
>
> **Waiting for Perfection** keeps many paralyzed, afraid to start until conditions are ideal. But purpose is discovered in progress, not perfection. If you wait until you feel completely ready, you may never begin.

>**Cultural Pressures** push us toward definitions of success that may not align with God's purposes. Society values prestige, wealth, and influence, while God often works through humility, sacrifice, and service. Discerning your purpose requires distinguishing between cultural expectations and divine calling.
>
>**Comfort Zones** are perhaps the most insidious obstacles to purpose. Familiar routines, even unfulfilling ones, feel safer than the unknown territories of purpose. Yet growth and impact happen beyond the boundaries of comfort. Whose idea was the 'comfort zone' anyway? Why can't we decide that the world is our comfort zone and experience every little piece of it.

Discerning Your Purpose

How do you discover God's specific purpose for your life? Here are some guideposts for the journey:

>**Spiritual Gifts** provide clues to your purpose. Holy Spirit has equipped you with specific abilities for building up the body of Christ (1 Corinthians 12:7). Whether teaching, encouragement, leadership, mercy, or other gifts, this divine enablement often indicate where God is calling you to serve.
>
>**Passion** signals purpose. What causes, needs, or opportunities ignite your enthusiasm? What problems do you feel compelled to solve? What injustices move you to action? The things that consistently kindle your passion often align with your purpose.
>
>**Experience** shapes your purpose. God wastes nothing—not even painful experiences. Your trials, successes, failures, and unique life journey have equipped you with perspectives and wisdom that others may not possess. These experiences are often preparation for your purpose.

Confirmation comes through multiple sources. Scripture, prayer, wise counsel, circumstances, and the inner witness of Holy Spirit should align to confirm your purpose. Be cautious of a "calling" that cannot be verified through these channels.

Fruitfulness validates purpose. When you're operating in your God-given purpose, there will typically be fruit—not necessarily immediate success, but evidence of God's hand at work. This fruit might include personal growth, positive impact on others, and glory brought to God.

Practical Steps to Finding Your Purpose

Here's how to step into your purpose:

1. **Seek God's Guidance** – Spend time in prayer, asking God to reveal His purpose for your life. Psalm 25:12 promises, "Who is the man who fears the LORD? Him will he instruct in the way that he should choose." God is more eager to reveal your purpose than you are to discover it.

2. **Use Your Gifts** – God has given you unique talents. Identify them and use them for His glory. As you serve faithfully in small ways, larger purposes often emerge. Don't despise humble beginnings or seemingly insignificant opportunities to use your gifts.

3. **Take Small Steps** – Purpose is often revealed through action. Start where you are and trust God for the next step. You don't need to see the entire staircase to take the first step. Each act of obedience illuminates more of the path ahead.

4. **Overcome Fear** – Fear will try to keep you stagnant. Choose faith over fear. Remember that God has not given us a spirit of fear but

of power, love, and a sound mind (2 Timothy 1:7). When fear whispers "what if you fail?" faith responds "what if you fly?"

5. **Surround Yourself with Encouragement** – Align yourself with people who will support your journey. Proverbs 13:20 says, "Whoever walks with the wise becomes wise." Find mentors who are walking purposefully with God and learn from their example.

6. **Trust the Process** – God's timing is perfect. Delays do not mean denial. Just as a seed must develop roots before producing fruit, your purpose may require seasons of hidden growth before visible impact. These waiting periods aren't wasted—they're essential to your development.

7. **Be Willing to Grow** – Purpose is refined over time. Embrace learning and new experiences. Remain teachable and humble, recognizing that God often adjusts our understanding of our purpose as we mature spiritually. What you're called to at 25 may evolve by 45 or 65.

Living Purposefully in Every Season

Purpose isn't just for the future—it's for today. Whatever season you're in, God has meaningful work for you to do:

In seasons of preparation, like David tending sheep before becoming king, focus on character development and skill building. These "backstage" seasons lay the foundation for future impact.

In seasons of waiting, like Joseph in prison, practice faithfulness in small things. God is often doing His deepest work when progress seems slowest.

In seasons of transition, like the Israelites in the wilderness, stay close to God's presence. When everything around you is changing, He remains the stable center that gives meaning to your journey.

In seasons of fulfillment, like Solomon building the temple, practice gratitude and humility. Remember that purpose fulfilled is a gift from God, not merely the result of your efforts.

In seasons of hardship, Jeremiah prophesying during national decline, choose resilience and hope. Some of God's most significant purposes unfold through difficulty and suffering.

Exiting Hell Moment

You are standing at a crossroads. One path leads to comfort and familiarity while the other leads to purpose and impact. God is calling you down the second path. Will you take the step? The familiar path may seem safer, but the purpose path leads to the fullness of life Jesus promised—a life of meaning, impact, and joy even amidst challenges.

Doubt and fear can create a personal hell that keeps you from your purpose. Today, step forward in faith. *Exhale* uncertainty and *inhale* divine direction.

The prison of purposelessness is one of life's most subtle torments—a quiet desperation that comes from knowing you were made for more but settling for less. Today, break free from that prison. Stop asking "Why am I here?" and start declaring "For this I was created!" The door is already unlocked; you need only the courage to walk through it into the spacious place of purpose God has prepared for you.

Affirmation

God has created me with divine purpose woven into the very fabric of my being. I choose to walk boldly in His calling for my life, embracing the truth that I am His masterpiece, intentionally designed for specific good works that He prepared in advance for me to accomplish with His strength and for His glory.

Action Step/Journal Prompt

Write down one step you can take today to move closer to your purpose. It can be as simple as reaching out to a mentor, signing up for a class, or dedicating time to prayer and reflection. Then, create a "purpose timeline." List significant moments in your past where God's hand was evident, note where you are now in your journey, and write down where you believe He is leading you. Review this timeline regularly as a reminder of God's faithful guidance in your life.

Day 23: The Power of Your Words - Creating Your Future

Scripture Focus

"Death and life are in the power of the tongue, and those who love it shall eat the fruit thereof." — Proverbs 18:21

Reflection

The words we speak are not merely sounds we make or letters we write. Words are creative forces that shape our reality. When God created the universe, He did so with words: "Let there be light." When Jesus performed miracles, He often spoke them into existence: "Lazarus, come forth." Throughout Scripture, we see a powerful truth: words precede reality. What you consistently speak today is forming the landscape of your tomorrow.

In Genesis 1, God didn't think the world into existence—He spoke it. Image-bearers of God, our words carry the same creative capacity. The words you speak are not neutral; they are either constructing or deconstructing your future. They are either aligning with God's promises or with the enemy's lies. In other words, the life you live today is the sum total of the words you spoke yesterday. If you want a different tomorrow, speak different words today.

The Creative Force of Words

Your words are your servants, going out to do your will. Your words shape your future in many ways, here are three:

> First, **they direct your focus**. Whatever you speak about repeatedly is what your mind gives attention to—whether positive or negative. Jesus taught that "out of the abundance of the

heart the mouth speaks" (Matthew 12:34). The reverse is also true. What your mouth speaks repeatedly will eventually fill your heart. When you constantly verbalize worry, fear, or inadequacy, you're training your mind to locate evidence that supports these negative narratives. Conversely, when you speak faith, possibility, and God's promises, your mind begins to recognize opportunities aligned with these truths.

Second, **they influence your emotions**. Neuroscience confirms what Scripture has always taught us: our words affect our internal state, our feelings and emotions. When you verbalize gratitude, you activate brain circuits associated with well-being. When you speak hopeful words about your future, your body responds with reduced stress hormones. Your words aren't just describing your emotions—they're creating them.

Third, **they impact your actions**. What you say to and about yourself and your future directly influences what you believe is possible, which then determines your behavior. If you consistently say, "I'll never get out of this situation," you'll likely take few, if any, steps toward change. But when you declare, "God has made a way where there seems to be no way," you begin to look for that way, take risks, and position yourself for breakthrough.

The Three Dimensions of Word Power

To fully harness the creative power of your words, give attention to these three areas:

1. **Your Internal Dialogue** – Some of us just need to be more kind to ourselves. The things we say to ourselves, we would never say to others. The conversations you have with yourself shape your perception and your expectations. This silent narrative often runs on autopilot, reinforcing old patterns and limitations. Some are even fueled by things others have said.

Whatever the case, begin by becoming aware of your self-talk. What messages do you repeatedly tell yourself? Are they aligned with God's truth about you? Paul instructs us to "take every thought captive to make it obedient to Christ" (2 Corinthians 10:5). Especially the words you say to yourself when no one else is listening.

2. **Your Spoken Declarations** - The words you speak aloud carry power. There's something about audibly declaring truth, saying things in your own hearing, that solidifies it in your spirit. Job lamented, "What I feared has come upon me." (Job 3:25) He verbalized his fears until finally, they manifested. Instead, follow David's example. As a young man, David was faced with the huge giant Goliath, that many grown men had run away from in fear. He declared to Goliath, "This day the LORD will deliver you into my hands." (1 Samuel 17:46) before the victory was realized. He spoke this aloud for everyone to hear, including the cowards cowering in the corner. You know the end of the story. With one smooth stone, David knocked Goliath clean out! Your spoken declarations are prophecies over your own life.

3. **Your Community Conversations** - The words you exchange with others creates a shared atmosphere that influences everyone involved. The Bible tells us "For where two or three gather in my name, there am I with them." (Matt. 18:20) Proverbs, the Book of Wisdom, warns that "the companion of fools will suffer harm." (Proverbs 13:20) More succinctly, foolish conversation creates foolish outcomes. Be intentional about the verbal environments you participate in. Do your conversations with others focus on problems or solutions? Complaints or possibilities? Gossip or edification?

Practical Applications for Word Transformation

Here's how to begin using your words to create the future God intends for you:

1. **Audit Your Current Word and Thought Patterns** - For one full day, pay close attention to your language patterns. What phrases do you repeat often? What tone characterizes your speech? What future are these words creating? Where does your language contradict God's promises or your desired future. I am an overthinker at times. I must audibly shout, "STOP" to get out of that cycle.

2. **Scriptural Declarations** - Identify specific promises from God's Word that address your current challenges and desires for the future. Craft these into first-person, present-tense declarations: "I am more than a conqueror through Christ who strengthens me." (Romans 8:37) Write these on cards to keep visible throughout your day.

3. **Institute Pattern-Breaking Phrases** - When you catch yourself speaking negatively, have ready responses to break the pattern. For example, if you find yourself saying, "I always mess this up," immediately counter with, "I'm learning and growing every day" or "that's not like me." If you're serious about breaking cycles, put a rubber band on your wrist and anytime you say something negative or contrary to God's Word, snap yourself. You will train yourself, in short order, to speak more positively than negatively.

4. **Speak to Your Mountains** - Jesus taught us to speak directly to our obstacles: "Say to this mountain, 'Move from here to there,' and it will move." (Matthew 17:20, NIV) Begin addressing your challenges directly with faith-filled words:

"Financial lack, you do not define my future. God is my source and my provider. Abundance is coming to me now."

5. **Join a Faith-Speaking Community** - Surround yourself with people who speak life rather than death. Find a prayer partner or small group where the conversation consistently aligns with God's promises rather than the world's limitations.

6. **Practice Prophetic Gratitude** - Begin thanking God for breakthroughs before they manifest. This isn't pretending—it's acknowledging that in the spiritual realm, your answer exists already. Your gratitude pulls future blessings into present reality.

Exiting Hell Moment

Your words are building materials—they construct the world you will inhabit tomorrow. Just as God spoke into the void and created the cosmos, your words are speaking into the void of your future, creating either limitations or possibilities.

Consider Joseph, who held onto the dream God gave him despite his circumstances. Even in a prison cell, he maintained a language of hope and divine purpose. He didn't speak like a prisoner, but like a person of destiny. And eventually, his words aligned with his reality when he was elevated to leadership.

Imagine if Moses had continued to say, "I cannot speak well" instead of accepting God's promise to be with his mouth. Imagine if Gideon had persisted in declaring "I am the least in my father's house" rather than embracing God's name for him: "Mighty Warrior." Their futures—and the future of Israel—hinged on their willingness to align their words with God's perspective rather than their own limitations.

The future you desire may seem distant, but it begins to form the moment you speak it with faith. This isn't magical thinking or mere positive confession—it's spiritual principle. God's Word declares that faith is "the substance of things hoped for, the evidence of things not seen" (Hebrews 11:1). Your faith-filled words begin to give substance to your hopes, creating evidence of realities not yet visible to the natural eye.

Starting today, speak as if your desired future—the one aligned with God's will for you—is already unfolding. Don't speak from your current limitations but from your future position. Don't talk about what you're leaving behind; talk about what you're moving toward. Your words should not merely describe where you are but should call forth where you're going.

Every word you speak is like a seed planted in the garden of tomorrow. What are you planting today? Doubt, fear, and limitation? Or faith, hope, and possibility? The harvest of your future depends on the seeds of your words today.

The hell of negative self-talk and destructive speech patterns is a prison with no locks—only the illusion of confinement. Today, recognize that you've been given the key of word-power. Your mouth is the doorway to your future. Step through it by speaking life, blessing, and divine possibility over yourself and your circumstances. **Exhale** words of defeat and **inhale** the language of victory.

Affirmation

My words create my reality, carrying divine power to shape circumstances and transform situations according to what I declare. I choose to speak life, blessing, and victory over my future with unwavering conviction, knowing that what I proclaim in faith today becomes my manifested reality tomorrow through God's faithful promise-keeping power.

Action Step/Journal Prompt

Write down three current situations in your life where you've been speaking negatively or from a perspective of limitation. For each situation, create three powerful declarations based on Scripture that paint a different future. Commit to speaking these declarations aloud three times daily for the next week, and journal any shifts you notice in your perspective, emotions, or circumstances.

Day 24: God Will Restore What You Lost - Participating in Restoration

Scripture Focus

"I will restore to you the years that the locust hath eaten, the cankerworm, and the caterpillar, and the palmerworm, my great army which I sent among you."
— Joel 2:25

Reflection

While the promise of Joel 2:25 assures us that God will restore what was lost, this restoration involves our active participation. Restoration is not just something God does for us—it's something He does with us. God invites us to collaborate with Him in the rebuilding process, bringing beauty from ashes and joy from mourning.

In the original context of Joel 2:25, God wasn't just promising to magically replace what the locusts had devoured. He was calling the people to return to Him with all their hearts (Joel 2:12), to consecrate themselves (Joel 2:16), and to prepare for restoration through repentance and renewed commitment. The promise of restoration comes with an invitation to participate in the process.

Understanding Divine Restoration

God's restoration goes beyond replacement—it involves transformation. When God restores, He doesn't merely return what was lost; He often provides something better, deeper, and more aligned with His purpose. When you think of transformation, think of the caterpillar transforming into a butterfly. The caterpillar becomes something it has never been before. That's our goal.

Consider Job, who lost everything—his wealth, his children, his health, and his reputation. When God restored Job, He gave him "twice as much as he had before." But the restoration wasn't automatic or immediate. It came after Job had wrestled with profound questions, encountered God in a new way, and prayed for the very friends who had misjudged him. Job participated in his restoration through faithfulness, perseverance, and forgiveness.

The full depth of restoration often includes:

1. **Recovery** - Getting back what was lost or receiving its equivalent

2. **Redemption** - Finding purpose and meaning in the loss itself

3. **Renewal** - Experiencing a refreshed perspective and approach to life

4. **Reimagination** - Receiving something that transcends what was lost

Your Role in the Restoration Process

While God is the ultimate restorer, there are specific ways you can participate in your restoration journey:

1. **Embracing the Grieving Process and the Pain of Recovery**

    Restoration begins with honestly acknowledging what was lost and the role you played in creating the problem. Before you can fully receive what, God wants to give you, you must process the reality of what was taken. This isn't about dwelling in the past but about honoring your experience. Part of the honesty necessary to overcome is realizing that it will be painful. Embrace the pain in the process knowing that healing is on its way.

King David modeled this when he "strengthened himself in the LORD his God" (1 Samuel 30:6) after finding his family taken and his city burned. He wept until he had no more strength to weep—then he turned to God for direction. His honest grief preceded his miraculous restoration.

2. Releasing Expectations About the Form of Restoration

We miss restoration because we're looking for an exact replacement of what we lost, while God has provided something different but better. The Israelites nearly missed their Messiah because He didn't come in the form they expected.

Release preconceived notions about how God should restore you. The widow of Zarephath (1 Kings 17) thought she was preparing her last meal before death. She could never have imagined that her act of generosity toward Elijah would result in supernatural provision that far exceeded what she had lost. The way God uses your challenges to advance you on your path to purpose is completely up to Him. Trust Him, trust the process and see the salvation of the Lord.

3. Practicing Prophetic Gratitude

Restoration often begins with thanking God for what He will do before you see evidence of it. This isn't denial or pretending; it's faith that acknowledges God's promises are as good as fulfilled.

When Jesus stood before Lazarus's tomb, He thanked God for hearing Him before Lazarus emerged (John 11:41-42). His gratitude preceded the miracle. Similarly, your thankfulness creates spiritual space for restoration to manifest.

4. Taking Redemptive Action

God often uses our hands to deliver His restoration. When the exiles returned to Jerusalem, they didn't just pray for walls to appear—they rebuilt them, stone by stone (Nehemiah 3). What practical steps can you take toward restoration? Perhaps it's developing a new skill, investing in a new relationship, seeking counseling, or creating something beautiful. These actions don't replace God's work; they participate in it.

5. Becoming a Channel of Restoration for Others

One of the most powerful ways God restores us is by making us agents of restoration for others. Joseph's path to restoration included becoming the channel through which an entire region, including his own family, was saved from famine.

As 2 Corinthians 1:3-4 reminds us, God "comforts us in all our troubles, so that we can comfort those in any trouble with the comfort we ourselves receive from God." Your wounds, once healed, qualify you to help heal others.

Restoration in Every Dimension

God's restoration touches every dimension of our lives:

Material Restoration may include finances, opportunities, possessions, or physical health. While God sometimes restores these things directly, He often provides wisdom, favor, and opportunities that require our stewardship.

Relational Restoration might involve reconciliation where possible, but also includes new relationships that fulfill the needs the broken relationships once met. God may restore your capacity to trust, love, and be vulnerable again.

Emotional Restoration addresses the internal wounds of betrayal, rejection, or loss. God heals these wounds through His presence, His Word, and often through the care of others who become His hands and voice in your life.

Purpose Restoration rekindles your sense of calling and meaning. What the enemy meant to derail your destiny, God uses to refine and clarify it. Like Joseph, your pit and prison become preparation for your palace.

Spiritual Restoration might be the most profound of all. Many testify that their deepest losses led to their richest communion with God. As David wrote in Psalm 51:12, "Restore to me the joy of your salvation." Sometimes what God most wants to restore is our first love for Him.

The Timeline of Restoration

God's restoration rarely follows our preferred timeline. Some restorations happen suddenly—a dramatic reversal, an unexpected opportunity, a miraculous provision. More often, restoration unfolds gradually, with small evidence of God's faithfulness that accumulate over time.

The Israelites' return from Babylonian exile illustrates this truth. Their restoration occurred in waves—first under Zerubbabel, then Ezra, then Nehemiah. The temple wasn't rebuilt in a day, nor the walls in a week. Each stage required faith, patience, and perseverance.

Your restoration may follow a similar pattern. Don't despise the day of small beginnings (Zechariah 4:10). Each step forward, however modest, is evidence of God's restoring work in your life.

Restoration as Testimony

As your restoration unfolds, it becomes one of your most powerful testimonies. Others looking at your life will see not just what you lost, but what God restored—and how He did it through your partnership with Him.

This is why Joel 2:26-27 follows the promise of restoration with these words: "You will have plenty to eat, until you are full, and you will praise the name of the LORD your God, who has worked wonders for you... Then you will know that I am in Israel, that I am the LORD your God, and that there is no other."

Your restoration isn't just for you—it's a witness to God's faithfulness that will strengthen others facing similar losses.

Exiting Hell Moment

The hell of irretrievable loss whispers that what's gone is gone forever—that the locust has had the final word in your story. Today, partner with God in believing and acting as if restoration has already begun. Because it has. ***Exhale*** despair over what was lost and ***inhale*** anticipation for what is coming. Step out of the prison of permanent loss into the open field of divine restoration, where God is already at work turning your mourning into dancing.

Affirmation

God has restored everything I've lost with divine creativity that transforms absence into abundance. I am not merely receiving His restoration but actively participating in it, watching with wonder as what was meant to destroy me becomes the unshakable foundation for greater blessing and breakthrough that exceeds what I had before.

Action Step/Journal Prompt

Identify one specific loss in your life that you're asking God to restore. Write down three practical steps you can take this week to participate in that restoration process. Then, write a prayer of prophetic gratitude, thanking God for the restoration as if it's already complete. Finally, consider one person you could reach out to who has experienced a similar loss—how might your story, even in its unfinished state, offer them hope?

Day 25: Embracing Your New Identity

Scripture Focus

"Therefore, if anyone is in Christ, the new creation has come: The old has gone, the new is here!" — 2 Corinthians 5:17

Reflection

When you leave behind old relationships, patterns, and seasons, you make space for a new identity to emerge. This isn't about reinventing yourself through your own efforts; it's about embracing who you already are in Christ. No matter what labels others have placed on you or what you've believed about yourself, God sees you through His lens of redemption and transformation.

God specializes in giving people new identities. He changed Abram to Abraham, Sarai to Sarah, Jacob to Israel, and Simon to Peter. Each name change signified a shift in identity and purpose. Similarly, when you accept Christ, you receive a new identity—beloved child of God, heir with Christ, ambassador of reconciliation, and more.

Your True Identity in Christ

Understanding who you are in Christ is essential to moving forward in wholeness:

- **You are Completely Forgiven** – "In him we have redemption through his blood, the forgiveness of sins, in accordance with the riches of God's grace" (Ephesians 1:7). Your past mistakes don't define you.

- **You are Deeply Loved** – "See what great love the Father has lavished on us, that we should be called children of God! And that is what we are!" (1 John 3:1). God's love for you is unconditional and unchanging.

- **You are Eternally Significant** – "For we are God's handiwork, created in Christ Jesus to do good works, which God prepared in advance for us to do" (Ephesians 2:10). You have a unique purpose and value.

- **You are Completely Accepted** – "To the praise of his glorious grace, which he has freely given us in the One he loves" (Ephesians 1:6). You don't have to earn approval.

- **You are Never Alone** – "And surely I am with you always, to the very end of the age" (Matthew 28:20). God's presence is your constant companion.

Letting Go of False Identities

Many of us carry false identities formed by painful experiences, others' opinions, or our own mistakes. These might include labels like "unlovable," "failure," "unwanted," "not enough," or "damaged goods." These labels are lies that contradict your identity in Christ.

Releasing these false identities involves:

1. **Recognize.** Recognizing the source – Is this identity from God or from another source? If it contradicts Scripture, it's not from God.

2. **Renounce.** Renouncing the lie – Actively reject identities that don't align with God's truth about you.

3. **Replace.** Replacing with truth – Fill your mind with Scripture that affirms your identity.

4. **Reinforce.** Reinforcing through practice – Intentionally live from your new identity, making choices that align with who God says you are.

Living from Your New Identity

Embracing your identity in Christ isn't just about knowing the right information—it's about living from this new reality. Here's how to practice your true identity:

1. **Start your day with identity affirmations** – Begin each morning by declaring who you are in Christ.

2. **Make decisions based on your true identity** – When facing choices, ask, "What would someone who knows they are God's beloved child do?"

3. **Surround yourself with truth-tellers** – Build relationships with people who see you through God's eyes and remind you of your true identity.

4. **Restructure your environment** – Remove items, relationships, or habits that reinforce old identities and introduce elements that remind you of your new identity.

5. **Serve from your identity, not for your identity** – Let your actions flow from who you already are, not from trying to prove your worth.

Embracing the Journey of Transformation

Your identity in Christ is both immediate and progressive. The moment you trust Christ; you become a new creation. Yet living into the fullness of this identity is a lifelong journey. Romans 12:2 encourages us to "be transformed by the renewing of your mind," indicating an ongoing process.

Just as a butterfly must struggle out of its chrysalis to strengthen its wings, your transformation may include challenges that ultimately strengthen your new identity. Be patient with yourself in this process. Transformation doesn't happen overnight, but with each choice to believe and live from your true identity, you become more fully who God created you to be.

Exiting Hell Moment

Imagine standing before a mirror, but instead of seeing your reflection through the lens of past hurts or failures, you see yourself through God's eyes—precious, purposed, and profoundly loved. This vision isn't wishful thinking; this is the most accurate reflection there is of who you truly are.

The prison of false identity keeps you trapped in patterns of thinking and behavior that don't reflect who God says you are. Today, step out of that confinement into the spacious freedom of your true identity in Christ. **Exhale** the labels others have placed on you, the mistakes that have defined you, and the lies you've believed about yourself. **Inhale** the truth of who you are—God's masterpiece, created anew for relationship with Him and impact in His kingdom.

Affirmation

I am a new creation in Christ, completely transformed as the old has gone and the new has gloriously come. I embrace my unshakable identity as God's beloved child, walking confidently in the freedom of being fully for

Day 25: Embracing Your New Identity

given, unconditionally loved, and purposefully designed for a divine calling that only I can fulfill.

Action Step/Journal Prompt

Write three false identities or labels you've carried. Next to each one, write the truth about who you are in Christ that counters that false identity, include the corresponding Scripture. Create a daily practice of declaring these truths over yourself. Then, identify one practical way you can live from your true identity today—a conversation, decision, or action that reflects who you really are in Christ.

Day 26: Building a Hopeful Future

Scripture Focus

"For I know the plans I have for you,' declares the LORD, 'plans to prosper you and not to harm you, plans to give you hope and a future."
— *Jeremiah 29:11 (NIV)*

Reflection

Hope, fueled by faith, is the power that moves us forward when the road gets tough. It's not wishful thinking or blind optimism; biblical hope is a confident expectation based on God's character and promises. As you stand at this threshold between what was and what will be, hope enables you to look forward with anticipation rather than anxiety.

God spoke the words of Jeremiah 29:11 to His people during their Babylonian exile—a season of profound loss and disorientation. Even in their darkest moment, God assured them that His plans and purposes were good. Similarly, whatever loss or transition you've experienced or are currently experiencing, God has already worked through, weaving hope and possibility into your future.

The Biblical Foundation of Hope

Throughout Scripture, hope emerges as a central theme:

- **Hope is an Anchor** – "We have this hope as an anchor for the soul, firm and secure" (Hebrews 6:19). When life feels stormy and uncertain, hope stabilizes us.

- **Hope does not Disappoint** – "And hope does not put us to shame, because God's love has been poured out into our hearts through

Holy Spirit, who has been given to us" (Romans 5:5). God-centered hope will never leave us embarrassed or let down.

- **Hope is connected to Faith** – "Now faith is confidence in what we hope for and assurance about what we do not see" (Hebrews 11:1). Hope and faith work together, giving substance to what we cannot yet see.

- **Hope is Cultivated in Community** – "May the God of hope fill you with all joy and peace as you trust in him, so that you may overflow with hope by the power of Holy Spirit" (Romans 15:13). Hope grows as we encourage one another.

Dreaming with God

Building a hopeful future involves partnering with God to dream new dreams. This isn't about imposing your plans on God, it's about aligning your hopes and dreams with His purposes.

Consider Joseph, whose dreams seemed shattered when his brothers sold him into slavery. Yet through every hardship, Joseph maintained hope in God's faithfulness. Eventually, he saw how God wove even painful experiences into a beautiful tapestry of purpose: "You intended to harm me, but God intended it for good to accomplish what is now being done, the saving of many lives" (Genesis 50:20).

What dreams is God placing in your heart? What passions, gifts, and opportunities might He be aligning to create your next chapter? Remember that God often plants the seeds of your future in the soil of your present circumstances.

Practical Steps for Building Your Future

Here are concrete ways to partner with God in building a hopeful future:

1. **Envision Possibilities** – Take time to imagine what could be, not limited by past disappointments. Ask God to expand your vision of what's possible.

2. **Set Faith-filled Goals** – Create specific, measurable goals that stretch your faith. Don't make your goals realistic, make them faith-filled. Realism is for those who lack faith. Write them down and review them regularly.

3. **Take Intentional Action** – Break down your goals into small, manageable steps. Progress comes through consistent action, not dramatic leaps.

4. **Cultivate Resilience** – Expect obstacles and setbacks as part of the journey. Develop strategies for bouncing back from disappointment while keeping your eyes fixed on God's promises.

5. **Surround Yourself with Hope-builders** – Connect with people who nurture hope in your life and distance yourself from those who consistently sow doubt, negativity and discouragement.

6. **Stay Grounded in Gratitude** – Regularly practice thankfulness for what God has already done. Gratitude for the past fuels hope for the future.

7. **Remain Flexible** – Hold your plans loosely, allowing God to redirect and refine them. Sometimes His path to your destination looks different than you expected.

Overcoming Obstacles to Hope

Even as you build toward a hopeful future, you may encounter internal and external obstacles:

> **Fear** whispers "What if you fail?" or "What if you're hurt again?" Counter fear with faith, remembering that God is with you in success and failure alike. Failure is simply you learning how something doesn't work.
>
> **Past disappointments** can make you hesitant to hope again. Acknowledge the pain of previous letdowns while recognizing that your future is not determined by your past.
>
> **Comparison** steals hope by focusing your attention on others' journeys rather than your own. Keep your eyes on your unique path and purpose.
>
> **Impatience** grows when transformation seems slow. Remember that meaningful change takes time—a day at a time, a step at a time.

With each obstacle you overcome, your capacity for hope grows stronger. What once seemed impossible begins to look inevitable as you walk with God.

Hope as a Spiritual Discipline

Cultivating hope is a spiritual practice that grows stronger with use. Just as you might exercise your physical muscles, you can strengthen your "hope muscle" through consistent practice:

- **Study Hope in Scripture** – Create a collection of verses about hope that you can turn to in challenging moments.

- **Speak Hope-filled Words** – Your language shapes your reality. Practice speaking words of possibility and expectation rather than doubt and defeat.

- **Celebrate Signs of Hope** – Notice and acknowledge even small evidence of God's work in your life and circumstances.

- **Share Hope with Others** – Hope multiplies when shared. Look for opportunities to encourage others with the hope you've received.

Exiting Hell Moment

You're standing at the threshold of a new chapter. Behind you lies what was—perhaps marked by pain, disappointment, or loss. Before you stretch what will be—yet to be written, full of possibility. In this pivotal moment, you choose hope, not because the path ahead is clear, but because you know the One who walks beside you. With each step forward, the future becomes clearer, brighter, and more beautiful than you could have imagined.

The prison of hopelessness convinces you that your future will merely be a repeat of your past—that nothing can or will change. Today, step out of that dark confinement into the light of hope. *Exhale* despair, cynicism, and resignation. *Inhale* possibility, purpose, and divine potential. Your future is not determined by what has happened to you but by the God who goes before you, making a way where there seems to be no way.

Affirmation

My future is filled with hope because God holds it in His hands, orchestrating every detail with perfect wisdom and unfailing love. I trust His good plans for my life with unshakable confidence, moving forward with bold assurance in His faithfulness that has never failed and will continue to guide me toward the abundant destiny He has prepared.

Action Step/Journal Prompt

Create a "Hope Board" for your future. This could be a physical poster board, digital document, or journal page. Include words, images, and Scriptures that represent the future you're building with God. Include both specific goals and the qualities or experiences you want to characterize your life (joy, purpose, healthy relationships, etc.). Place your Hope Board where you'll see it daily as a reminder of the future God is preparing.

Finally, identify one small step you can take this week toward this hopeful future, and commit to taking that step.

Day 27: Walking in Confidence - Living in Divine Assurance

Scripture Focus

"Being confident of this very thing, that he which hath begun a good work in you will perform it until the day of Jesus Christ." — Philippians 1:6

Reflection

True confidence isn't something we manufacture through positive thinking or self-help strategies. It's a deep, unshakable assurance that flows from understanding who God is and who we are in Him. This divine confidence transforms every aspect of how we navigate life—from decision-making to relationships, from handling adversity to pursuing purpose.

The difference between worldly confidence and godly confidence is foundational. Worldly confidence is built on shifting sand—accomplishments, appearances, abilities, or approval from others. Divine confidence, however, is anchored in the unchanging character of God and our identity as His beloved children. It doesn't fluctuate with circumstances because its source is eternal.

The Paradox of Confidence in Weakness

One of the most powerful paradoxes in Scripture is that true confidence often emerges from acknowledged weakness. Paul wrote in 2 Corinthians 2:9-10, "Therefore I will boast all the more gladly about my weaknesses, so that Christ's power may rest on me... For when I am weak, then I am strong."

Rather than being a contradiction, this is a divine principle. When we recognize our limitations and dependency on God, we access His limitless power. Unlike self-confidence, which relies on our own resources, God-confidence draws from an infinite well of divine provision.

Consider Moses, who initially protested, "Who am I that I should go to Pharaoh?" (Exodus 3:11). His confidence didn't come from believing in himself, but from believing in the God who promised, "I will be with you" (Exodus 3:12). Moses' weakness became the canvas on which God's strength was displayed.

Confidence in Divine Identity

At the core of walking in confidence is settling the question of identity. Said otherwise, when you know who you are, who you are is settled. Many of us struggle with confidence because we're unsure of who we truly are. We define ourselves by our families, our worst failures, others' opinions, or fleeting accomplishments. Divine confidence, however, rests in an identity that can't be earned, taken away, or diminished by circumstance.

In Christ, you are:

1. **Unconditionally Loved** - "I have loved you with an everlasting love." (Jeremiah 31:3)

2. **Fully Forgiven** - "As far as the east is from the west, so far has he removed our transgressions from us." (Psalm 103:12)

3. **Eternally Secure** - "No one can snatch them out of my Father's hand." (John 10:29)

4. **Divinely Purposed** - "Created in Christ Jesus to do good works, which God prepared in advance for us to do." (Ephesians 2:10)

5. **Continuously transformed** - "We all... are being transformed into his image with ever-increasing glory." (2 Corinthians 3:18)

When your confidence is rooted in who God says you are rather than in fluctuating circumstances or the opinions of others, you develop an unshakable foundation that withstands life's storms.

The Language of Confidence

Confidence has its own vocabulary and syntax. It speaks differently than insecurity or pride. The language of divine confidence is characterized by:

Humble Certainty - "I can do all things through Christ who strengthens me." (Philippians 4:13) Notice this isn't "I can do all things because I'm amazing" but rather a recognition of the source of strength.

Future-oriented Expectation - "We are more than conquerors through him who loved us." (Romans 8:37) Confidence speaks about victory before it materializes in the natural realm.

God-centered Perspective - "If God is for us, who can be against us?" (Romans 8:31) Confidence continually references God's power, promises, and presence rather than personal abilities or favorable circumstances.

Resilience in Setbacks - "Though the fig tree does not bud... yet I will rejoice in the LORD." (Habakkuk 3:17-18) Confidence isn't deterred by temporary obstacles but sees beyond them to God's faithfulness.

As you adopt this language—both in your self-talk and in your conversations with others -- your mind gradually aligns with these truths, and confidence becomes your default orientation rather than an occasional visitor.

Confidence in Action

Confidence isn't just an internal state; it manifests in tangible behaviors. Walking in confidence means:

Making decisions without being paralyzed by fear - Confident people aren't reckless. They don't allow "what ifs" to immobilize them. They seek wisdom, then move forward, trusting God with outcomes they can't control. They feel the fear and do the task anyway.

Setting healthy boundaries - Divine confidence enables you to say "no" without guilt and "yes" without resentment. You understand your value doesn't depend on pleasing others or earning their approval.

Taking appropriate risks - The confident person steps out of comfort zones not from reckless bravado but from trust in God's guidance. Like Peter stepping out of the boat, they focus on Jesus rather than the waves.

Receiving both criticism and praise with equilibrium - Confidence gives you the ability to learn from criticism without being devastated by it and to appreciate praise without becoming dependent on it. To do both, we use a principal called deflection.

Speaking truth with grace - Confident people don't need to dominate conversations or aggressively assert their views. They can express convictions clearly and quietly while respecting others' perspectives.

Admitting mistakes and weaknesses - Perhaps counterintuitively, confident people readily acknowledge errors and limitations because their worth isn't tied to perfection.

Developing Confidence Through Spiritual Disciplines

Divine confidence doesn't typically arrive as an instantaneous gift; it develops over time and through intentional spiritual practices:

Scripture Meditation transforms your thinking by replacing lies with truth. When you regularly immerse yourself in God's Word, His perspective gradually becomes your default worldview.

Prayer Cultivates Intimacy with God, moving you from theoretical knowledge about Him to experiential knowledge of Him. This relationship becomes the bedrock of your confidence.

Testimony Remembrance builds faith for the future by recalling God's faithfulness in the past. Keep a record of God's interventions in your life and review it regularly, especially in challenging seasons.

Community Confirmation provides external reinforcement for internal conviction. Surround yourself with people who see you through God's eyes and remind you of your true identity when you forget.

Obedient Action strengthens confidence through experience. Each step of obedience, regardless of outcome, builds spiritual muscle memory that makes the next step easier.

Worship Shifts Focus from your limitations to God's unlimited power. Regular worship recalibrates your perspective, reminding you of the vastness of the God in whom your confidence rests.

Confidence in Seasons of Waiting

Perhaps the greatest test of confidence comes in seasons of waiting, when God's promises seem delayed and His presence feels distant. During these times, confidence isn't the absence of questions but the presence of trust despite those questions.

Consider Abraham, who "against all hope, in hope believed" (Romans 4:18) during the long wait for his promised son. His confidence wasn't in what he could see but in who God is—faithful to His Word and able to do the impossible.

In your own waiting seasons, confidence means continuing to act as if God's promises are true and manifested even when evidence seems lacking. It means refusing to resort to human shortcuts like Abraham did with Hagar, trusting instead in God's perfect timing and methods.

Overcoming Confidence Killers

Several forces actively work against divine confidence:

> **Past failures** whisper that you'll always repeat the same mistakes. Confidence counters with the truth that in Christ, you're a new creation being transformed daily.
>
> **Comparison** steals confidence by focusing on others' strengths versus your weaknesses. Confidence remembers that you're running your own race, uniquely designed and equipped by God.
>
> **Perfectionism** sets impossible standards that guarantee a sense of failure. Confidence embraces growth as a process, celebrating progress rather than demanding perfection.

Rejection suggests your value depends on others' acceptance. Confidence rests in God's unwavering acceptance that never fluctuates based on performance or popularity.

Catastrophic thinking imagines worst-case scenarios that paralyze forward movement. Confidence acknowledges real risks but focuses on God's presence in every potential future.

From Confidence to Impact

The ultimate purpose of divine confidence isn't personal comfort or achievement—it's Kingdom impact. When you walk in genuine confidence, you become a conduit for God's power to flow through you into a world desperate for hope.

Joshua's confidence allowed him to lead a nation into their promised inheritance. Esther's confidence empowered her to approach the king uninvited and save her people. Paul's confidence enabled him to plant churches across the Roman Empire despite relentless opposition.

Your confidence matters not just for your own well-being but for the divine assignments that await you. Someone needs the gift, message, or ministry that only a confident you can deliver.

Exiting Hell Moment

You stand at the edge of your next challenge, not with arrogance or self-sufficiency, but with a quiet, unshakable assurance that the God who called you will equip you. You move forward, not in your own strength, but in His, knowing that whatever the outcome, His purpose will prevail. This is divine confidence—not the absence of obstacles but the presence of God in the midst of them.

The prison of insecurity keeps you small, hiding your gifts and shrinking from opportunities. But God has called you to live boldly—not with pride or presumption, but with humble confidence in His ability to work through you. Today, step out of the shadows of self-doubt into the light of God's truth about who you are and what you're capable of through His strength. Your insecurity is not humility; it's unbelief dressed in religious clothing. True humility acknowledges both your limitations and God's limitless power available to you. **Exhale** the lie that you're not enough and **inhale** the truth that Christ in you is more than sufficient.

Affirmation

I walk in divine confidence, not because of who I am, but because of whose I am—a treasured child of the Most High God. His power works mightily through my weakness, His perfect wisdom guides my every decision, and His unfailing love secures my identity beyond all doubt. I move forward boldly in His purposes, fully assured that the One who called me is absolutely faithful to complete the magnificent work He has begun in me.

Action Step/Journal Prompt

Identify three areas where insecurity has prevented you from stepping into God's purposes. For each area, write down a biblical truth that counters that specific insecurity. Then, choose one concrete action step you can take today that requires divine confidence. It might be having a difficult conversation, pursuing an opportunity, using a gift, or making a decision you've been postponing. After taking that step, journal what you learned about God's faithfulness and your growing confidence.

Day 28: Enter God's Rest – Establishing Sacred Rhythms

Scripture Focus

"There remains, then, a Sabbath-rest for the people of God; for anyone who enters God's rest also rests from their works, just as God did from his." — Hebrews 4:9-10 (NIV)

Reflection

Rest is not merely the absence of activity—it is a sacred posture of the soul. In our hyperactive, achievement-oriented culture, true rest has become one of the most countercultural and spiritually revolutionary acts available to believers. To enter God's rest is to step into a different dimension of living, one that operates according to divine rhythms rather than human striving.

Rest is not a luxury for the spiritually elite but a necessity for every believer. God's rest is both a present reality we can experience daily and an eternal promise we anticipate. It's not something we achieve through effort but something we receive through surrender.

The Biblical Foundation of Rest

Rest has been part of God's design from the beginning. In Genesis 2:2-3, God rested on the seventh day, not because He was tired, but to establish a pattern for human flourishing. This wasn't merely a pause in activity but a celebration of completion—a holy punctuation that gave meaning to the work that preceded it.

Throughout Scripture, we see God's consistent invitation to rest:

- In Exodus 20:8-11, rest becomes codified in the Ten Commandments as Sabbath observance

- In Psalm 23:2-3, David speaks of God making him "lie down in green pastures" and "restoring his soul"

- In Matthew 11:28-30, Jesus offers rest for the weary and burdened

- In Hebrews 4:1-11, the writer elaborates on the deeper spiritual rest available to believers

These passages reveal that rest isn't just about physical recuperation but spiritual realignment. It's about remembering who is really in control (God, not us) and what truly matters (being, not just doing).

The Dimensions of Divine Rest

God's rest operates in multiple dimensions:

> **Physical Rest** involves giving your body the recovery it needs. This isn't laziness—it's stewardship of the temple God has given you. In a culture that glorifies exhaustion and busyness, choosing physical rest is an act of faith that acknowledges your human limitations.

> **Mental Rest** means allowing your mind to detach from problem-solving, planning, and worrying. It's creating space for your thoughts to settle, your creativity to renew, and your perspective to widen. Practices like meditation on Scripture, nature walks, or even mindful silence can facilitate mental rest.

Emotional Rest is giving yourself permission to process feelings rather than suppressing or being controlled by them. It involves releasing burdens to God, practicing forgiveness, and finding safe spaces to be emotionally authentic.

Spiritual Rest is perhaps the deepest form—ceasing from self-salvation efforts and resting in Christ's completed work. This means surrendering the exhausting pursuit of earning God's favor or proving your worth.

Relational Rest involves setting healthy boundaries, being authentic rather than performing, and cultivating connections that energize rather than drain you.

The Obstacles to Entering Rest

Despite God's clear invitation to rest, many believers struggle to enter it fully. Several barriers commonly prevent us from experiencing this divine gift:

The Productivity Idol measures human worth by output and achievement. This cultural value is so ingrained that rest often triggers guilt or anxiety. We must recognize and reject the lie that our value comes from what we produce.

Digital Distraction keeps our minds constantly stimulated and engaged. The endless scroll, the always-on connectivity, and the fear of missing out prevent the deep stillness necessary for true rest. Rest requires intentional disconnection from these digital demands.

Misplaced Identity causes us to seek validation through performance. When who we are is confused with what we do, rest feels threatening to our very sense of self.

2. Weekly Sabbath Observance

There is transformative power in reclaiming a weekly Sabbath—a full day set apart for rest, worship, and relationship:

- **Preparation** - A restful Sabbath requires preparation. Complete necessary tasks beforehand so you're not tempted to work on your day of rest.

- **Protection** - Guard your Sabbath from encroachments by setting clear boundaries around work, media consumption, and activities that drain rather than replenish.

- **Presence** - Make your Sabbath about being fully present with God, yourself, and others, not just abstaining from work.

- **Pleasure** - Include elements of delight and joy. God's rest isn't austere or boring; it's filled with the good gifts He wants you to enjoy.

3. Seasonal Retreats

Beyond weekly rhythms, consider incorporating extended periods of rest throughout the year:

- **Quarterly Personal Retreats** - Set aside at least a weekend each quarter for deeper reflection, evaluation, and renewal.

- **Annual Spiritual Retreats** - Once a year, if possible, take a full week for more substantive disconnection and reconnection with God.

- **Sabbaticals** - For those in ministry or intense seasons of service, consider longer sabbaticals every 7-10 years for deeper restoration.

4. Life Season Awareness

Different seasons of life require different approaches to rest:

- **High-Demand Seasons** may allow only for minimal rest practices, but these become even more essential during such times.

- **Recovery Seasons** following burnout or trauma may require more intensive rest as part of the healing process.

- **Transitional Seasons** between major life changes benefit from intentional rest to process endings and prepare for new beginnings.

The Paradoxical Productivity of Rest

True rest doesn't diminish our effectiveness—it exponentially increases it. When we enter God's rest, we experience:

Clearer Perspective. Rest creates distance that allows us to see situations more objectively and prioritize more wisely.

Renewed Creativity. Many breakthrough ideas and solutions emerge not during active problem-solving but in moments of rest when our minds can make new connections.

Deeper Discernment. In the quiet of rest, we can better distinguish God's voice from competing voices, leading to more Spirit-led decisions.

Greater Resilience. Regular rest prevents burnout and builds capacity to handle challenges with grace rather than reactivity.

Authentic Presence - Rested people can be fully present with others rather than physically present but mentally elsewhere.

The Ultimate Rest

All our earthly rest practices point toward and provide a foretaste of the ultimate rest promised in Revelation 21-22—the perfect fellowship with God for which we were created. Every Sabbath, every quiet moment, every release of burden into God's hands is rehearsal for eternity.

This eternal perspective transforms how we view rest—not as an interruption of our important work but as a glimpse of our ultimate destination. As Augustine famously wrote, "Our hearts are restless until they rest in You." Our souls long for this rest because we were made for communion with God.

Exiting Hell Moment

The hell of perpetual striving keeps you on a treadmill of exhaustion, always running but never arriving. Today, step off that treadmill into the spacious freedom of God's rest. *Exhale* the weight of self-sufficiency. *Inhale* the peace of divine sufficiency. The prison doors of workaholism, perfectionism, and performance-based identity are already unlocked— Jesus opened them through His finished work. All that remains is for you to walk through them into the rest He has already secured for you.

Affirmation

I enter God's rest not as an escape from responsibility but as an embrace of my true identity as His beloved child. I cease striving and know that He is God, finding profound peace in the truth that my value lies not in what I produce but in who I am. In stillness and trust, I discover my strength divinely renewed for every purpose He has ordained.

Action Step/Journal Prompt

This week, establish one concrete rest practice in each dimension of rest (physical, mental, emotional, spiritual, and relational). For example, you might schedule a specific time for physical exercise and recovery, implement a digital sunset each evening for mental rest, journal about a difficult emotion for emotional rest, spend time in worship for spiritual rest, and have an authentic conversation with a trusted friend for relational rest.

Additionally, plan one full Sabbath day this week. Prepare for it by completing necessary tasks ahead of time. Decide what you will set aside (work, certain technologies, etc.), and what you will embrace (worship, nature, relationships, etc.). After experiencing this Sabbath, journal about what you noticed, how it affected your relationship with God, and how you might refine this practice moving forward.

Day 29: Breaking Chains and Moving Forward – Walking in Sustained Freedom

Scripture Focus

"It is for freedom that Christ has set us free. Stand firm, then, and do not let yourselves be burdened again by a yoke of slavery." — *Galatians 5:1 (NIV)*

Reflection

Freedom is an ongoing journey, not a one-time event. While the chains of bondage may be broken in a moment of divine intervention, most of the time, it is a process of getting free. Learning to walk in sustained freedom requires intentional practices, renewed thinking, continuous surrender and a level of discipline most of us cannot muster. As we approach the conclusion of our 31-day journey, it's vital to understand how to maintain and deepen the freedom you've begun to experience.

The Apostle Paul's warning in Galatians 5:1 acknowledges a sobering reality: it's possible to be set free and then return to bondage. Freedom requires not only an initial breaking of chains, it also requires a daily decision to "stand firm" in that liberation. Many have experienced breakthrough moments only to gradually slip back into old patterns. It's not normally a huge, earth-shattering revelation. It typically starts with an occasional "I can handle it" and before you know it, it becomes more detrimental than the previous issue. The chains you thought were broken have reappeared only this time, many times worse.

The Anatomy of Spiritual Chains

To maintain freedom, we must first understand the nature of the chains that once bound us. Spiritual bondage typically involves three interconnected components, mindsets, soul ties and strongholds:

> **Mindsets** are deeply ingrained ways of thinking that shape how we interpret reality. These might include victim mentality, perfectionism, scarcity thinking, or catastrophizing. Even after external circumstances change, these mindsets can persist, creating internal chains that limit our freedom.
>
> **Soul Ties** are unhealthy emotional and spiritual connections that continue to influence us long after a relationship or situation has ended. These attachments act like invisible cords, pulling us back toward former bondages.
>
> **Strongholds** are fortified thought patterns where the enemy has established territory in our minds. As 2 Corinthians 10:4-5 describes, these fortresses must be demolished through spiritual warfare, not merely human effort.

Breaking Chains at Their Source

Lasting freedom comes from addressing the roots, and not just the fruit of the challenge, not just the symptoms of bondage but their root causes. Like a gardener who removes weeds by the roots rather than merely cutting off what's visible above ground, we must identify and uproot the sources of our chains:

> **Lies We Have Chosen to Believe** often form the foundation of bondage. These might be lies about God (He doesn't really love me), about yourself (I'm unworthy of love), or about others (No one can be trusted). Freedom begins as these lies are identified and replaced with truth. One of the biggest lies that we believe is that

we are a product of our environment. We act as if we cannot be better because our family has certain attributes when we are free from the curse of our law and generational bloodlines. Decide and instead, choose to believe you are better, you are free, you are saved from the curse of the law.

Ungodly Soul Agreements are internal vows or agreements we've made in response to pain or fear. "I'll never be vulnerable again," "I must be perfect to be accepted," or "I don't deserve good things" are examples of agreements that create self-imposed chains.

Generational Patterns can transmit bondage across family lines. While we aren't responsible for the sins of our ancestors (Ezekiel 18:20), we can be affected by familial patterns that create a propensity toward certain struggles. Breaking generational chains of ten requires identifying, renouncing, and replacing these inherited tendencies.

Traumatic Experiences can create chains of fear, shame, or self-protection that persist long after the danger has passed. Freedom from trauma-based chains often requires both spiritual ministry and therapeutic support.

The Process of Sustained Freedom

Freedom is both an event and a process—a gift received and a discipline developed. Here's how to nurture the freedom Christ has given you:

1. **Maintain a Freedom Mindset**

    Your thinking patterns are either fortifying your freedom or undermining it. Romans 12:2 instructs us to "be transformed by the renewing of your mind." This transformation involves:

Meditating on Scripture Meditations rewire your thinking according to God's truths. Choose key verses related to your specific area of bondage and incorporate them into daily review.

Prayer is your lifeline and spiritual reset. This is your time to go deeper in communion with God – listening, repenting and receiving. These conversations with God are not just emotional outlets, they are the power source of transformation.

Thought Awareness and Capture as described in 2 Corinthians 10:5. Practice noticing when thoughts arise that contradict God's truth and deliberately replace them with biblical affirmations.

Strategic Declarations that align your spoken words with God's promises. What you consistently declare shapes what you ultimately believe and experience.

Freedom-Focused Community that reinforces new thinking patterns. Surround yourself with people who see you as God sees you and speak truth when old mindsets resurface.

2. **Establish Freedom Practices**

Freedom is maintained through consistent spiritual disciplines that strengthen your connection to God and weaken the influence of former bondages:

Regular Spiritual Inventory allows you to identify warning signs of returning bondage. Set aside time weekly to honestly assess your thoughts, emotions, and behaviors.

Accountability Relationships provide external perspective and support. Choose trustworthy individuals who will ask difficult questions and speak truth in love.

Worship as Warfare shifts your focus from chains to the Chain-Breaker. Regular worship reminds you of God's power and presence, making former bondages lose their appeal.

Serving Others reinforces your freedom by allowing you to partner with God in others' liberation. As you help others break free, your own freedom deepens.

3. **Navigate Freedom Challenges**

   Even with right thinking and spiritual practices, challenges to your freedom will come. Preparing for these challenges ensures they won't derail your progress:

   Recognize Triggers that make old bondages appealing. These might be certain relationships, environments, stressors, or emotional states that previously led to destructive patterns.

   Develop Response Plans for moments of vulnerability. Don't wait until you're tempted to decide how you'll respond. Establish in advance what steps you'll take when triggers arise.

   Practice Immediate Realignment when you momentarily step back into old patterns. The enemy wants a temporary slip to become a complete return to bondage. Quickly acknowledge the misstep, receive forgiveness, and reestablish your commitment to freedom.

   Celebrate Progress rather than demanding perfection. Freedom grows through consistent direction, not flawless performance. Acknowledge and celebrate each victory, no matter how small.

Freedom's Ultimate Purpose

Please know that your chains being broken is not merely for your personal comfort or happiness. Freedom always has a greater purpose. Your freedom is designed to enable you to fulfill your divine calling, to walk in your God-breathed purpose, and as you are free, you can then extend liberation to others.

The Israelites weren't freed from Egyptian slavery merely to enjoy the absence of taskmasters. Their freedom was for them to become a kingdom of priests, a holy nation (Exodus 19:6). Similarly, your freedom has both personal and Kingdom implications.

Often, your freedom is designed to position you to create and attract resources to do God's will. As you walk in sustained freedom, ask: "What does this liberation enable me to do that I couldn't do before? How might God use my freedom story to help break chains in others' lives? Ask yourself, what calling can I now pursue that was previously hindered by bondage?"

Your testimony of maintained freedom becomes a powerful weapon against the enemy's deceptions. Revelation 12:11 reminds us that believers overcome "by the blood of the Lamb and by the word of their testimony." As you consistently walk in freedom, your life demonstrates that chains can be permanently broken, offering hope to those still bound.

Moving Forward with Purpose

Forward movement requires more than merely leaving bondage behind; it demands intentional steps toward God's purpose. Like the Israelites who needed to move toward Canaan rather than merely celebrating their exodus from Egypt, you must combine your freedom from bondage with movement toward destiny.

This involves:

Clarifying Divine Direction for this new season of freedom. Spend time listening to God's voice, studying His Word, and seeking wise counsel about your next steps.

Taking Sanctified Risks that stretch your faith. Freedom opens doors that fear previously kept closed. Walking through these doors often requires courage and calculated risk-taking.

Establishing New Patterns aligned with your new identity. Freedom feels disorienting when not accompanied by new routines and relationships that reinforce your liberated status.

Pursuing Purposeful Development of gifts, skills, and character qualities that equip you for your calling. Freedom creates space for growth that wasn't possible while bound.

Exiting Hell Moment

The hell of perpetual bondage convinces you that your chains, though occasionally loosened, will always eventually tighten again. Today, reject that lie and step into the truth that Christ has set you free, not temporarily, but permanently. The loosening of your chains was not a brief respite but the beginning of a lifetime of increasing liberty. *Exhale* resignation to recurring bondage and *inhale* faith for sustained freedom. The door to your prison cell hasn't just been cracked open—it's been removed from its hinges. Walk out boldly, knowing that with each forward step, you move further from captivity and closer to the spacious place God has prepared for you.

Affirmation

I am permanently free in Christ. My chains are broken, not merely loosened. I stand firm in my freedom, refusing to return to former bondages. Each day, I move forward in greater liberty, walking confidently in the purpose for which Christ has set me free.

Action Step/Journal Prompt

Create and execute on your "Freedom Maintenance Plan." Make sure it includes:

1. Three specific mindset shifts you need to embrace in order to sustain your freedom (e.g., from "I'll always struggle with this" to "Through Christ, I am permanently free").

2. Write three regular practices that you'll implement to strengthen your freedom (e.g., weekly accountability with a trusted friend, daily declarations of specific truths, regular service in an area related to your freedom). Schedule them into your calendar, with notifications, that you will not ignore.

3. Identify the primary triggers that send you back into bondage and develop a specific strategy to respond to each one.

4. Write a letter to your future self, reminding yourself of how far you've come and encouraging continued vigilance in maintaining your freedom.

5. Set a calendar reminder for one month from today to review your Freedom Maintenance Plan and assess your progress in walking in sustained liberty. Then set it again to ensure your progress continues.

Day 30: Celebrating Your Journey

Scripture Focus

"The LORD has done great things for us, and we are filled with joy." — *Psalm 126:3*

Reflection

Congratulations! You've completed thirty days of intentional growth, healing, and transformation. Today is a day to pause, reflect, and celebrate how far you've come. In our rush to reach the next milestone, we often forget to acknowledge the journey itself—the small victories, the lessons learned, and the growth that has taken place along the way.

Celebration is a spiritual practice found throughout Scripture. The Israelites regularly paused to commemorate God's faithfulness through feasts, memorials, and moments of corporate worship. Jesus attended weddings and celebrations, even performing His first miracle at a wedding feast. God delights when His children recognize and rejoice in His work in their lives.

The Power of Remembrance

Looking back and celebrating on your journey serves several important purposes:

- **Reinforces God's Faithfulness** – When you recall how God has sustained you through difficult times, your faith grows stronger for future challenges.

- **Highlights your Progress** – Change often happens so gradually that we don't notice it. Intentional reflection helps you recognize how far you've come.

- **Brings Closure to this Chapter and Propels you into a Future of Finishing** – Acknowledging what you've learned and how you've grown creates a sense of completion, even as you continue moving forward.

- **Fuels Gratitude** – Seeing God's hand at work in your journey naturally leads to thanksgiving, which cultivates joy, contentment, and continued progress.

Scripture often connects remembrance with rejoicing. Psalm 77:11-12 says, "I will remember the deeds of the LORD; yes, I will remember your miracles of long ago. I will consider all your works and meditate on all your mighty deeds." Remembering precedes rejoicing.

Milestones in Your Journey

Over these thirty days, you've explored numerous aspects of healing and growth. Take time to reflect on these milestones:

1. **Breaking Free from Unhealthy Patterns** – You've recognized destructive cycles and begun to establish new, life-giving habits.

2. **Embracing your True Identity** – You've moved from defining yourself by past hurts or relationships to seeing yourself through God's eyes.

3. **Finding Strength in Weakness** – You've learned that vulnerability before God is not weakness but the pathway to experiencing His power.

4. **Practicing Forgiveness** – You've begun the process of releasing bitterness and extending grace to yourself and others.

5. **Establishing Healthy Boundaries** – You've learned to protect what's precious while remaining open to authentic connection.

6. **Cultivating Spiritual Disciplines** – You've explored practices like prayer, Scripture meditation, and Sabbath that nurture your relationship with God.

7. **Building a Supportive Community** – You've recognized the importance of surrounding yourself with people who encourage your growth.

In which of these areas have you shown the most growth? Where have you experienced breakthrough? What surprised you about your journey?

Celebrating Your Progress

Celebration doesn't have to be elaborate to be meaningful. Here are some ways to honor your journey:

1. **Create a Tangible Reminder** – Make or purchase something that symbolizes this season of growth. It might be a piece of jewelry, artwork, or another meaningful item that reminds you of how far you've come.

2. **Share Your Story** – Tell someone you trust about your journey. Articulating your experience helps solidify what you've learned and might encourage someone else.

3. **Write a Letter to Yourself** – Capture what you want to remember from this experience. What would you tell your future self when challenges arise again?

4. **Plan a Personal Celebration** – Do something special just for you—a nice meal, an outing to a favorite place, or an activity that brings you joy.

5. **Practice Intentional Gratitude** – Make a list of specific moments during these thirty days when you experienced God's presence, guidance, or transformation.

Remember, celebration isn't about perfection — it's about progress. You don't need to have everything figured out to acknowledge how far you've come.

Learning from Setbacks

Your 30-day journey likely included not only victories but also challenges and even setbacks. These, too, are worth reflecting on—not to dwell in discouragement but to extract their valuable lessons.

The Apostle Paul wrote in Philippians 3:13-14, "But one thing I do: Forgetting what is behind and straining toward what is ahead, I press on toward the goal to win the prize for which God has called me heavenward in Christ Jesus." Importantly, "forgetting what is behind" doesn't mean ignoring the lessons of the past, but rather not allowing past failures to define or limit your future.

What setbacks did you experience during these thirty days? What did they teach you about yourself, about God, and about the healing process? How might these lessons equip you for the journey ahead?

Exiting Hell Moment

You stand at the top of a mountain, looking back at the path you've climbed. There were steep sections, unexpected turns, and moments you weren't sure you could continue. Yet here you stand, having persevered with God's help. The view from here grants perspective on just how far you've come. And though there are more mountains ahead, you face them with greater strength, wisdom, and confidence in the God who has been faithful every step of the way.

The hell of stagnation whispers that you'll always be stuck, that real change is impossible. But these 30-days have proven otherwise. Today, step fully out of that lie and into the truth of your ongoing transformation. *Exhale* discouragement about imperfect progress. *Inhale* celebration of the real growth that has occurred and continues to unfold.

Your journey of healing is both completed and continuing—celebrate how far you've come while embracing the path still ahead.

Affirmation

I celebrate my journey of healing and growth with profound gratitude for the transformation God has wrought in my life. The Lord has done great things for me, filling my heart with unmistakable joy that testifies to His faithful care. I continue forward in unshakable faith, fully confident in God's ongoing masterpiece unfolding in every area of my life.

Action Step/Journal Prompt

Create a personal celebration of your thirty-one-day journey:

1. First, review your journal entries or reflections from previous days, noting areas of growth and breakthrough.

2. Write a letter to yourself acknowledging specific ways you've changed and grown.

3. Do something tangible to mark this milestone—perhaps share a special meal with a friend, create a piece of art that represents your journey, or spend time in a place that feels meaningful to you. As you celebrate, express gratitude to God for His faithful presence throughout your journey.

Bonus Day 31: From Surviving to Thriving - Your Journey Continues

Scripture Focus

"The Lord will guide you always; he will satisfy your needs in a sun-scorched land and will strengthen your frame. You will be like a well-watered garden, like a spring whose waters never fail." — Isaiah 58:11

Reflection

Congratulations! We added a 31st day as a bonus!! You've actually completed a transformative 31-day journey from darkness into light, from bondage into freedom, from waiting to exiting. This milestone deserves recognition and celebration. The growth you've experienced isn't the end of your story—it's a new beginning. Today marks your transition from merely surviving to genuinely thriving in the abundance God has prepared for you.

Throughout this journey, you've encountered various aspects of growth and healing. You've learned to find strength in life's storms, to break free from chains that once bound you, to embrace God's rest, to walk in confidence, and to discover purpose even in pain. These aren't isolated lessons but interconnected threads in the beautiful tapestry God is weaving in your life.

The Integration of Your Journey

Life's storms reveal both God's strength and the resilience He has built within you. As we saw in Mark 4:35-41, when the disciples faced the raging sea, Jesus didn't just calm the external storm—He addressed their internal storm of fear. Similarly, your journey hasn't just been about changing your circumstances but transforming your heart and mind.

The woman who rebuilt her life after her business collapsed discovered that the storm didn't destroy her—it revealed strength she didn't know she had. The story about overcoming motorcycle fear showed how helping others can silence our own fears. These narratives illustrate a profound truth: your breakthrough isn't just for you—it's meant to become a blessing to others.

From Comfort to Comforter

One of the most beautiful progressions in the Christian journey is the movement from receiving comfort to becoming a source of comfort for others. As 2 Corinthians 1:3-4 reminds us, God "comforts us in all our troubles, so that we can comfort those in any trouble with the comfort we ourselves receive from God."

The pain you've experienced and overcome now qualifies you to minister to others in similar situations. Your story of exiting hell becomes a roadmap for someone else who's still waiting for their breakthrough. This is the divine multiplication of your healing—it doesn't just change your life but extends to transform others' lives as well.

Consider: Who around you might be facing the same storms you've weathered? Who needs to hear that freedom is possible because you've experienced it firsthand? Your testimony isn't just a personal milestone; it's a powerful tool in God's hands to bring hope to those still waiting to exit their own personal hells.

Sustaining Your Progress

The journey you've begun these past 30 days requires ongoing attention to sustain and deepen. Freedom, confidence, purpose, and peace aren't destinations you arrive at once and for all—they're territories you learn to temporary measures but lifetime rhythms. Continue to prioritize these disciplines, adapting them to different seasons but never abandoning them. They are the soil in which your continued transformation will grow.

1. Maintain Godly Practices

The practices that have supported your growth—prayer, Scripture meditation, worship, journaling, rest—are not temporary measures but lifetime rhythms. Continue to prioritize these disciplines, adapting them to different seasons but never abandoning them. They are the soil in which your continued transformation will grow.

2. Guard Your Mindset

You've learned to replace lies with truth, doubt with faith, and fear with confidence. This renewal of your mind is an ongoing process. Remain vigilant against old thought patterns that may try to reassert themselves. As you've discovered, what you consistently think determines the direction of your life.

3. Cultivate Supportive Community

No one thrives in isolation. Surround yourself with people who reinforce your freedom rather than pull you back into bondage. Seek relationships that challenge you to grow while providing grace when you struggle. Be intentional about building connections with those who are further along in their journey and can mentor you, as well as those you can encourage.

4. Embrace Continuous Growth

The areas where you've experienced breakthrough may reveal new territories that need attention. As one layer of healing occurs, deeper layers often become evident. This isn't a sign of failure but of progress—like peeling an onion to reach its core. Welcome this new awareness as opportunities for deeper transformation rather than seeing them as setbacks.

5. Live From Purpose, Not Pain

As you move forward, let your decisions be guided by your God-given purpose rather than reactions to past pain. This shift from reactive to proactive living is one of the clearest signs of true healing. You're no longer defined by what happened to you but by what God is doing through you.

Your Unique Impact

No one else has your exact combination of experiences, insights, gifts, and calling. The journey you've traveled these 31 days has been uniquely yours, even if others have walked similar paths. This means your contribution to God's kingdom and to the lives of others around you is irreplaceable.

The woman who overcame her motorcycle fear found that helping someone else face their fears silenced her own. This beautiful paradox—that in lifting others, we ourselves are lifted—is at the heart of kingdom living. As Jesus taught, "Whoever wants to save their life will lose it, but whoever loses their life for me will find it" (Matthew 16:25).

What is the unique way God is calling you to "lose your life" for His purposes? How might your exit from hell become an entrance path for someone else's liberation? These questions aren't merely philosophical—they're practical invitations to deeper meaning and purpose.

Looking Forward: From Exit to Entrance

Exiting hell is significant, but it's only half the story. The Israelites' exodus from Egypt wasn't complete until they entered the Promised Land. Similarly, your freedom isn't just about what you've left behind but what you're moving toward.

Isaiah 58:11 paints a beautiful picture of this forward movement: "The Lord will guide you always; he will satisfy your needs in a sun-scorched land and will strengthen your frame. You will be like a well-watered garden, like a spring whose waters never fail." This promise speaks of continuous guidance, supernatural provision, and abundant fruitfulness—a life not just surviving but thriving.

The Ongoing Journey

While you've completed this thirty-day devotional, your journey of growth and transformation continues. The principles and practices you've explored aren't confined to a month-long program but are meant to become part of your ongoing walk with God.

As you move forward, consider:

- Which practices from these thirty days do you want to continue as regular rhythms in your life?

- What areas still need healing and attention?

- What is your next step in continued growth?

- Who will walk alongside you in the next phase of your journey?

Remember that transformation is both immediate and progressive. Some changes happen in an instant; others unfold over a lifetime. Be patient with the process while remaining committed to continued growth.

Exiting Hell Moment

The final hell to exit is the belief that your transformation has limits—that you can only heal so much, grow so far, or impact so many. Today, step out of that confining mindset into the limitless possibilities of a life fully surrendered to God. **Exhale** any remaining doubt about what God can do through your restored life and **inhale** the promise that "with God all things are possible" (Matthew 19:26). Your exit from hell was never the ultimate goal—it was just the necessary first step toward the abundant life Christ promised.

Affirmation

I am not just surviving; I am thriving with supernatural vitality that flows from the Author of life himself. My healing continues to deepen with each passing day, my freedom expands beyond previous limitations, and my life becomes a powerful channel of God's restoration to others who are still in darkness. What God has started in me; He has brought glorious completion with perfect faithfulness and divine precision.

Action Step/Journal Prompt

Take time to reflect on your entire 31-day journey.

1. Write a letter to yourself capturing the most significant insights, breakthroughs, and changes you've experienced.

2. Write a vision statement for your next season—not just what you want to do but who you want to become. Really give this some time and thought. Don't just ask AI for a response This is your life and the question deserves some time and meditation.

3. Identify one person who needs the hope your story can offer and make a specific plan to share your experience with them in a way that might illuminate their own path to freedom.

Conclusion: Stepping Boldly into Your New Beginning

As you reach the end of this 31-day journey, I want to remind you that this is not just the end of a book—it is the beginning of a new chapter in your life. You have taken the time to reflect, to break chains, to release burdens, and to embrace the transformation God has for you. Now, it is time to walk in the freedom, confidence, and peace that you have gained.

Exiting hell is not about a single moment—it is about a continual choice. There will be days when you feel strong and days when you feel weak. There will be moments when old fears try to creep back in, and times when the enemy whispers lie that make you question your progress. Remember, *you are not who you were when you started this journey*.

Each day of this process has built something inside of you—strength, wisdom, resilience, and faith. The trials that once held you down no longer have the same power over you because you now know where your true power comes from: **God's presence in your life.**

Here's an important truth—you will still face challenges. Life is not suddenly free from difficulties just because you have worked through this process. The difference is that now, you are equipped. You have tools. You have Scripture. You have a foundation of faith that will sustain you through anything.

Continue looking forward as The Journey Continues …

Affirmations by Phase

Phase 1: Initial Healing (Days 1-10)

Day 1: In Your Anger, Do Not Sin - *I am completely forgiven, gloriously redeemed, and radiantly free in Christ, walking in the fullness of grace that has broken every chain and washed away every stain of my past. The blood of Jesus has transformed me from a prisoner of shame into a beloved child of God, empowered by His Spirit to live victoriously today and face tomorrow with unshakable confidence in His unfailing promises.*

Day 2: Break Free from Guilt - *I am completely forgiven, gloriously redeemed, and radiantly free in Christ, walking in the fullness of grace that has broken every chain and washed away every stain of my past. The blood of Jesus has transformed me from a prisoner of shame into a beloved child of God, empowered by His Spirit to live victoriously today and face tomorrow with unshakable confidence in His unfailing promises.*

Day 3: The Power of Forgiveness - *I release bitterness and choose forgiveness, breaking free from the prison of resentment that once held my heart captive and poisoned my spirit. I am free to walk in the light of grace, unburdened by the weight of past hurts, empowered to embrace each new day with a heart cleansed by mercy and hope to the abundant joy that flows from choosing love over anger.*

Day 4: Finding Peace in the Chaos - *I receive God's perfect peace that flows like a river through every corner of my soul, washing away all anxiety and filling me with divine tranquility that the world cannot give or take away. My heart is at peace and I am not afraid, for I am securely held in the loving hands of my Heavenly Father who commands the wind and waves and whose powerful presence surrounds me with an unshakable calm even in life's fiercest storms.*

Day 5: Strength for the Weary - *The Lord renews my strength with divine power that infuses every fiber of my being, transforming my weakness into supernatural ability and my fatigue into heavenly energy that never depletes. I will soar on wings like eagles above life's challenges, run the race set before me without growing weary, and walk forward in unwavering faith that carries me through every valley and mountaintop with the steadfast assurance that my God goes before me, behind me, and beside me in every step of my journey.*

Day 6: God is not Finished With You - *I am alive and thriving because God is not finished with me yet, His divine purpose for my life unfolding with perfect timing and wisdom far beyond my limited understanding. Each breath I take declares His ongoing masterpiece within me, transforming my weaknesses into strengths, my trials into testimony, and my broken places into channels for His glory to shine through with breathtaking brilliance that testifies to His unfailing faithfulness and limitless love.*

Day 7: Choose Joy in the Midst of Pain - *The joy of the Lord is my strength, an inexhaustible wellspring of divine power that flows through me even in the darkest valleys and most challenging seasons of my journey. I choose joy today with unwavering determination, knowing that this supernatural gladness transcends my circumstances, defies my enemies, and connects my heart to the eternal delight of my Heavenly Father who rejoices over me with singing and whose presence fills my life with purpose and peace beyond all understanding.*

Day 8: Don't Contemplate What Might Have Been - *I choose to focus forward, not backward, releasing the weight of yesterday's failures and disappointments to embrace the limitless possibilities that lie ahead on the path God has prepared for me.*

Yesterday is gone. God's mercies are new every morning, cascading over me like a cleansing waterfall that washes away every stain of regret and renews my vision to clearly see the fresh work He is doing in my life today—a divine masterpiece unfolding with perfect timing and purpose that will transform my greatest challenges into my most powerful testimony.

Day 9: Finding Renewal When You're Weary - *The Lord renews my strength with divine power that surges through my entire being, replacing my exhaustion with supernatural energy and transforming my weakness into heaven-sent resilience that never diminishes. I will soar on wings like eagles above every obstacle that attempts to ground me, run the race marked out for me without growing weary or losing heart, and walk forward in unwavering faith that propels me through each valley and mountaintop with the absolute certainty that my God orchestrates every step of my journey for His glory and my ultimate good.*

Day 10: Cure Loneliness with Solitude - *Today, I will change my mindset, discarding limiting perspectives that have clouded my vision and embracing transformative truths that illuminate my path with clarity and purpose. I am not alone; I am enjoying my solitude—a sacred space where I discover the richness of my own company, hear God's voice with greater clarity, and cultivate the inner strength that prepares me for meaningful connection with others when the season is right.*

Phase 2: Inner Transformation (Days 11-20)

Day 11: God Will Restore All You Lost - *God has restored what I lost with divine precision and supernatural abundance, weaving together broken threads into a tapestry more beautiful than what was taken from me. He has made all things new in my life—not merely repairing what was damaged but creating something more glorious that reflects His redemptive power and unfailing love. What the enemy meant for harm, God has turned for my good and His glory, transforming my deepest wounds into channels of healing for others and my darkest valleys into platforms where His light shines with unmistakable brilliance that testifies to His sovereignty over every circumstance.*

Day 12: Trusting God's Timing - *God's timing is perfect, orchestrating every detail of my life with divine precision that transcends my limited understanding. I trust Him completely to make everything beautiful in its time, resting in the certainty that He weaves delays, detours, and even disappointments into a masterpiece of purpose that will ultimately reveal His glory and my good.*

Day 13: Embracing New Beginnings - *I am a new creation in Christ, completely transformed by His redeeming power that has erased my past and freed me from its grip. The old has gone and the new has come, infusing every part of my being with divine purpose and heavenly identity that cannot be diminished by circumstances or defined by my former failures.*

Day 14: Control Your Thinking - *I will not dwell on the past—for God is doing a new thing in me. I declare that fresh vision, fresh opportunities, and divine surprises are already unfolding in my life. What once felt dry and barren is now springing forth with purpose and possibility. I may not have seen it before, but now I choose to perceive it. My eyes are open, my heart is ready, and my spirit is* aligned. I embrace the new, the now, and the next with faith and expectation—because God has already begun!

Day 15: The Power of Your Words - *I am a new creation in Christ, completely transformed by His redeeming power that has erased my past and freed me from its grip. The old has gone and the new has come, infusing every part of my being with divine purpose and heavenly identity that cannot be diminished by circumstances or defined by my former failures.*

Day 16: God's Grace is Enough - *God's grace is sufficient for me. In my weakness, He is strong. I no longer need to strive for approval that has already been given through Christ.*

Day 17: Walking in Confidence - *I am confident in the Lord, standing firm in the knowledge that He has fully equipped me for my divine calling. I walk boldly in faith, not trusting in my limited abilities but in the almighty God who works powerfully within me, transforming ordinary efforts into extraordinary outcomes through His unlimited strength and perfect wisdom.*

Day 18: The Battle is the Lord's - *I trust God to fight my battles with perfect wisdom and sovereign power that far exceeds my own strength or strategy. I am not alone in my struggles, for the Creator of the universe stands beside me, working all things together for my ultimate good and ensuring that victory already belongs to Him before the battle even begins.*

Day 19: Breaking Chains and Moving Forward - *I am free in Christ, completely liberated from the chains that once held me captive to my past mistakes and limiting beliefs. I let go of what was and move forward in victory, knowing that what once bound me no longer defines me because I now walk confidently in the precious freedom that was purchased for me at the cross of Calvary.*

Day 20: Enter into God's Rest - *I am worthy of care and rest, embracing God's divine rhythm of Sabbath not as a luxury but as a sacred necessity for my soul's flourishing. I nurture myself with intentional self-care, honoring my Creator who designed renewal as essential to my purpose, and becoming more abundantly equipped to pour out authentic love to others from my replenished wellspring.*

Phase 3: Empowerment and Future (Days 21-31)

Day 21: Overcoming Fear with Faith - *I will not be ruled by fear. I choose faith, knowing that God has given me power, love, and a sound mind. I am not ruled by fear that seeks to paralyze my potential and distort my perspective. I choose faith with unwavering conviction, standing firmly on the truth that God has given me power to overcome, love that casts out all fear, and a sound mind that remains anchored in His unchanging promises regardless of what circumstances might suggest.*

Day 22: Stepping Into Your Purpose - *God has created me with divine purpose woven into the very fabric of my being. I choose to walk boldly in His calling for my life, embracing the truth that I am His masterpiece, intentionally designed for specific good works that He prepared in advance for me to accomplish with His strength and for His glory.*

Day 23: The Power of Your Words (Deeper Application) - *My words create my reality, carrying divine power to shape circumstances and transform situations according to what I declare. I choose to speak life, blessing, and victory over my future with unwavering conviction, knowing that what I proclaim in faith today becomes my manifested reality tomorrow through God's faithful promise-keeping power.*

Day 24: God Will Restore What You Lost (Deeper Application) - *God has restored everything I've lost with divine creativity that transforms absence into abundance. I am not merely receiving His restoration but actively participating in it, watching with wonder as what was meant to destroy me becomes the unshakable foundation for greater blessing and breakthrough that exceeds what I had before.*

Day 25: Embracing Your New Identity - *I am a new creation in Christ, completely transformed as the old has gone and the new has* *gloriously come. I embrace my unshakable identity as God's beloved child, walking confidently in the freedom of being fully forgiven, unconditionally loved, and purposefully designed for a divine calling that only I can fulfill.*

Day 26: Building a Hopeful Future - *My future is filled with hope because God holds it in His hands, orchestrating every detail with perfect wisdom and unfailing love. I trust His good plans for my life with unshakable confidence, moving forward with bold assurance in His faithfulness that has never failed and will continue to guide me toward the abundant destiny He has prepared.*

Day 27: Walking in Confidence (Deeper Application) - *I walk in divine confidence, not because of who I am, but because of whose I am—a treasured child of the Most High God. His power works mightily through my weakness, His perfect wisdom guides my every decision, and His unfailing love secures my identity beyond all doubt. I move forward boldly in His purposes, fully assured that the One who called me is absolutely faithful to complete the magnificent work He has begun in me.*

Day 28: Enter into God's Rest (Deeper Application) - *I enter God's rest not as an escape from responsibility but as an embrace of my true identity as His beloved child. I cease striving and know that He is God, finding profound peace in the truth that my value lies not in what I produce but in who I am. In stillness and trust, I discover my strength divinely renewed for every purpose He has ordained.*

Day 29: Breaking Chains and Moving Forward (Deeper Application) - *I am permanently free in Christ. My chains are broken, not merely loosened. I stand firm in my freedom, refusing to return to former bondages. Each day, I move forward in greater liberty, walking confidently in the purpose for which Christ has set me free.*

Day 30: Celebrating Your Journey - *I celebrate my journey of healing and growth with profound gratitude for the transformation*

God has wrought in my life. The Lord has done great things for me, filling my heart with unmistakable joy that testifies to His faithful care. I continue forward in unshakable faith, fully confident in God's ongoing masterpiece unfolding in every area of my life.

Day 31: From Surviving to Thriving - Your Journey Continues - *I am not just surviving; I am thriving with supernatural vitality that flows from the Author of life himself. My healing continues to deepen with each passing day, my freedom expands beyond previous limitations, and my life becomes a powerful channel of God's restoration to others who are still in darkness. What God has started in me; He has brought glorious completion with perfect faithfulness and divine precision.*

WOW PRAYER DAILY

There's no better way to begin your day than in His presence.

JOIN US IN PRAYER!

www.WOWMinistriesGlobal.org

www.ingramcontent.com/pod-product-compliance
Lightning Source LLC
Chambersburg PA
CBHW071943160426
43198CB00011B/1528